The Wedding Present

For Konstantia, without whom this book would never have been written, for my daughter Sarah who shared so closely in those wonderful discoveries in Greece, for my son Jamie and for George, Alexander and Xenia.

The Wedding Present

Riches of Spiritual Wisdom
for Life's Journey

Margaret Long

Gracewing.

First published in 1999

Gracewing
2 Southern Avenue, Leominster
Herefordshire HR6 0QF

UK ISBN 0 85244 5261

Typesetting by
Action Publishing Technology Ltd, Gloucester, GL1 1SP

Printed in England by MPG Books Ltd.,
Bodmin PL31 1EG

Contents

So if there is any encouragement in
Christ, any incentive of love, any
participation in the Spirit, any affection
and sympathy, complete my joy by being of
the same mind, having the same love ...
(Philippians 2.1–2)

I would like to thank not only those who have so kindly written letters of encouragement, and contributed in so many ways, but also the following who have put up with me through many months and encouraged me, whether through prayer or patience or affection or instruction:

Metropolitan Anthony of Sourozh, for giving his Blessing to this book.
Archbishop Gregorios of Thyateira and Great Britain, for his prayers and consistent encouragement.
John Tavener – my Orthodox Godfather (although much younger than me!)
Lilian (Delevoryas) and Robin Amis, Konstantia Pateras Woodruff, Diamantis Pateras, Nicholas Pateras, Ilyas Haritakis, Sister Frances of the Cross, Dr Edward and Mary Short, Father John Lee, Ian Dixon, Anna Tham, William Barlow, Father Meliton Oakes, Teresa de Bertodano, Jo Ashworth, Ron Collins, Father John Salter and Archimandrite Isaias Simonopetritis.

Preface

The idea of this book began with a request from Konstantia Pateras that I put some words from the Scriptures and from the Fathers into a notebook to be given to her as a wedding present. They were taken from a collection I had made during a period of severe testing when I had clung to them as though to a rock.

Most marriages will need to survive periods of testing and most of us encounter temptations and situations which threaten to come between us and God. So this book is for those who struggle to follow Christ in a world that continues to reject Him.

There is a strong Orthodox influence because of my own conversion to Orthodoxy which began in Greece. The excerpts are shorter than I would like. It is difficult to condense Orthodoxy, but I hope the glimpses that you find here might persuade you to delve deeper. I have included contemporary Western writers and passages from the Scriptures so that there will be familiar, uniting landmarks for those who are finding the Eastern Orthodox Tradition for the first time!

Many of the contributions are short and succinct. Others are longer. Some are for direct, immediate 'help' and some to make us think more deeply. Certain words will speak to you more than others, and many may grow on you, perhaps months after you first read them.

As Europe opens up, so the immense richness of the Orthodox Church and the writings of the early Fathers will seep into the West.

If I have any regrets it is that I discovered Orthodoxy so late. If I have any wish it is that the disciplines, the dignity and the beauty of this great tradition could help to bring the sense of the sacred back into the West.

Margaret Long

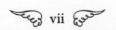

Foreword

The presence of our Lord at the Marriage of Cana was not a mere social call, for He was not just another guest invited there. He was the incarnate Son of the living God, in Whom the fullness of Divinity was embodied. Besides being a unique honour to the newlyweds, His presence was an event with profound and mystical significance. It was by itself a blessing and a sacrament. It was a testimony that the old things gave place to the new and redeemed order of life. His presence was the gift He brought to the newlyweds and to all couples who 'in the Lord' exchange marital vows. With Him a new element entered the realm of human life: the grace of God, which is the invisible factor in all the sacraments of our Church.

So wrote a predecessor of mine in the see of Thyateira and Great Britain, Archbishop Athenagoras (Kokkinakis) of blessed memory; and although he was writing about the Sacrament of Marriage [in *Parents and Priests as Servants of Redemption* (New York, 1958) p. 61], this extract bears a certain parallel to *The Wedding Present* – the anthology that Margaret Long began putting together at the request of Konstantia Pateras, a book that is both the result of prayer and which induces prayer.

This rich collection of spiritual quotations, collected under various headings and developing her chosen themes in a natural and unforced way, is drawn from a variety of traditions which usually homes in on the author's own Orthodox Faith and is indeed a 'gift'. It is a gift both for the newlyweds for whom it was intended but also for all of us in our spiritual quest as we seek to draw near to the Divine Bridegroom who 'humbled Himself, and became obedient unto death, even the death of the Cross',

(*Phil 2:8*) that through His Resurrection we might become participants in 'the new and redeemed order of life'.

This is a book whose paragraphs are to be slowly savoured. In the rich bouquet of extracts collected here, one feels the presence of God pervading the environment. In the quietness and privacy of one's room, the Triune God draws near, not on 'a mere social call' but in the 'fullness of Divinity'. From the 'profound and mystical' wealth contained here, God's presence is indeed 'a blessing and a sacrament', conferring His Grace. The written word on the page becomes a prayer welling up from the depths of the soul – sometimes challenging, always encouraging.

This 'Present' is one for all men and women who belong to the Body of Christ through confessing Him and are thereby united with Him and in Him. It is a 'Present' to bless this union, in which 'with Him, a new element (has) entered the realm of human life: the grace of God, which is the invisible factor in all the sacraments of our Church', as it is of life itself.

Praying for all of you, who will surely find in these pages a 'place of light, a place of green pasture, a place of refreshment', and especially for Margaret Long who has shown such tenacious dedication to producing this anthology and who has put so much effort into compiling this labour of love.

I remain,

With blessings and love in Christ

Gregorios
Archbishop of Thyateira
and Great Britain

Introduction

The Church is like a woman
With the face of a young girl,
And the white hair of wisdom.

ST HERMAS
(Early disciple of Christ)

This is for me, the perfect description of the Orthodox Church. And what I find so moving about Margaret Long's book, is the fact that the book itself is a living icon of St Hermas' words. We in the West live in a vast intellectual junkyard, largely brought about by a forgetfulness of the spontaneous, the intuitive, revealed theology, and a forgetfulness of 'SOPHIA', the Divine feminine principle.

The women stood by the cross of Christ/God — Christ appeared to Mary Magdalene — indeed the Church *is* 'feminine' — just look at the exquisite domes of Byzantine Churches.

In her book, Margaret Long takes the words of the Fathers, and then 'theologizes' them, not in a 'scholastic' way, but with all the tenderness and loving care of a mother. I remember a Greek monk saying to me once that we must first 'become' the Mother of God, before we are able to 'bear' Christ within us. The Incarnation is of course the ultimate strategy of Divine Love, because by becoming a human being the Word is able to replace the Law as external command.

These are my spontaneous reactions to a first reading of *The Wedding Present* — more like a relationship in progress, than a state of being.

JOHN TAVENER

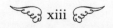

A Russian Orthodox Wedding

My daugher Sarah was married in the Russian Orthodox Cathedral in London. People often ask how, and why it is different from our Western Church.

Prayer in the Russian Church is a spiritual phenomenon which is little known in the West. To understand it you really need to experience it from the inside for there is a complex interweaving of themes. In contrast I remember going to a summer Anglican wedding, where there were reports on the current cricket scores from the vicar. And jokes. You won't find that in an Orthodox Church. There is an unhurried holiness and beauty. It is a manifestation of spiritual beauty – you see and feel it even if you cannot describe it – yet 'it is the only true way of deciding what is Orthodox and what is not.'

The Orthodox wedding is more than a brief exchange of legality – it is a journey into wisdom and knowledge with profound spiritual blessings, using, whether in English, Slavonic or Greek, the immense power and poetry of language.

Amid the stillness of the icons and candlelight the couple embark on a journey. This is the timeless feel of Orthodoxy, you move from the outside world into a sacred place where the Laws of God's Kingdom are being established on earth. In the Cathedral the sound of the Russian choir comes from the gallery. It is beautiful and unearthly, ascetic rather than sentimental – as though joining Heaven to earth.

As the marriage service proceeds emphasis is not so much on legal promises, but on God's grace. Divorce is not approved of in the Orthodox Church, but it is allowed. Man is fallible. God is forgiving. The journey begins in the Old Testament, the love and authority of God moving

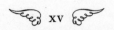

through the ancient geneology of the Bible, reminding us of our roots. Abraham and Sarah, Isaac and Rebecca, Zacharias and Elisabeth ... 'As thou wert present there, so likewise be thou present here, with thine invisible protection.' By the end of the very long geneology and powerful prayers one is made to feel the loving Fatherhood and authority of God. More awe-inspiring than anything man could devise.

The marriage continues with prayers expressed with this ancient, heady poetry of the Scriptures ... 'a crown of glory which fadeth not away. Preserve their bed unassailed, and give them of the dew of heaven from on high, and of the fatness of the earth. Fill their houses with wheat, and wine and oil, and with every beneficence, that they may bestow in turn upon the needy ... Exalt them like the cedars of Lebanon, like a luxuriant vine. Give them seed in number like unto the full ears of grain: that, having sufficiency in all things, they may abound in every work that is good and acceptable unto thee. And let them behold their children's children, like a newly planted olive orchard, round about their table; that, obtaining favour in thy sight, they may shine like the stars of heaven, in thee, our God.'

The couple move on their journey to Christ's first miracle in Cana. They are given a cup to drink from and the golden crowns are held over the heads of the Bride and Bridegroom. There are more prayers of abundant blessing: 'O God, our God, who didst come to Cana of Galilee, and didst bless there the marriage feast: Bless, also, these thy servants, who through thy good providence are now united together in wedlock. Bless their goings out and their comings in; replenish their life with good things, receive their crowns into thy kingdom, preserving them spotless, blameless, and without reproach, unto ages of ages.'

The Bride and Bridegroom are then crowned, as King and Queen of their own Kingdom, in Christ.

> Like the Wedding, this book is about our mystical journey, sometimes happy, sometimes hazardous — but with God's wisdom and benevolence always available, as we move towards His Kingdom.

Starting the Journey

My sheep hear my voice, and I know them, and they follow me; and I give them eternal life, and they shall never perish, and no-one shall snatch them out of my hand.

(JOHN 10.27)

We shall not seek to understand in order that we may believe, but to believe in order that we may understand. Hence we shall not seek for proof that God is wise. The unbelieving mind would not be convinced by any proof, and the worshipping heart needs none.

A.W. TOZER

The Knowledge of the Holy

Stand at the cross roads, and look; ask for the ancient paths, ask where the good way is; and walk in it ...

(JEREMIAH 6.16)

We have lived off the outside of our faith for too long ... maybe what we have got to learn is to return to the depth of faith.

DR GEORGE CAREY
Archbishop of Canterbury

In order to depict our Christian path more clearly, let us adopt the method of the Fathers and make an analogy. When we look at an ancient tree reaching high up to the clouds, we know that its roots, deep in the ground, must be correspondingly powerful. If the roots did not stretch down into the dark depths of the earth, as deep, perhaps, as the tree is high, if the mass and strength of the roots did not parallel the size and weight of the visible part of the tree, they could not nourish the tree or keep it upright – the lightest breeze would blow it down. So it is in man's spiritual life.

ARCHIMANDRITE SOPHRONY
We Shall See Him as He is

Whatever He Saith Unto You, Do it

It is never too late to receive God's call. Abraham was 75, Moses was 80 and Noah was 500 years old! But of course it is simpler to know Him as early as possible before setting out on our pilgrimage so that we can avoid too many detours and wrong turnings, 'for His Word is a Lamp to our feet and a light to our path.' (Psalm 119.105)

It may be difficult to comprehend that God has a plan for our lives, for each one of us. Yet it is stressed how wonderfully we are made – it was no accident for 'Thou didst form my inward parts, thou didst knit me together in my mother's womb.' (Psalm 139.13)

We only have to think for a moment about the stars, the birds, the trees and every flower from the rose to the bluebell – each so perfectly designed and yet so different. And each one with its place in the glory of Creation. As we think about this we begin to realize that we too have our purpose, and our differences, and even our disabilities, are part of that purpose.

Fear or anguish, or simply curiosity about why we exist at all may precipitate our search, and we may have to start our journey in blind faith. But as Isaac of Nineveh tells us, 'Faith is the doorway to the Mysteries'. And gradually we surrender to God's guidance as He speaks to us from His Sacred Word in the Scriptures, as He shows us His Creation, and as He reaches us in the silence of prayer. We know that it is a very personal love that He has for us and that there is a definite plan for our lives and a definite path for us to follow. His love is intimate. Nothing is haphazard. He has known us from the beginning.

O Lord Thou has searched me and known me,
Thou knowest when I sit down and when I rise up,
Thou discernest my thoughts from afar
Thou searchest out my path ... and art acquainted with all my ways.

(Psalm 139.1–3)

Cardinal Basil Hume suggested we stand the word 'searching' on its head. 'It helps if we switch from the notion of our searching for God and instead think about God coming to find us, for after all, that is the way it is. It is we who are lost. It is God who is looking for us.' However, we will never understand what good is up against if we do not understand evil. As Christians we cannot pretend that evil does not exist for the battle with evil is integral to our faith.

The clearest theological description I have ever heard was from Nicky Gumbel speaking on the Alpha Course. He describes the Garden of Eden (Genesis 2) as Permission, Prohibition and Penalty.

The garden with its figurative language was filled with beautiful trees from which to eat. There was plenty of choice in this beautiful place. Only one tree was forbidden, the tree of the knowledge of good and evil – 'for in the day you eat of it you shall die.' But they doubted God. And then we see the Penalty and the consequences after they had eaten the forbidden fruit. First there was shame and embarrassment. Then they hid from God. Their relationship with God was broken. And thirdly, they blamed each other. The man blamed the woman, the woman blamed the serpent and the serpent as has been said, didn't have a leg to stand on!

The consequences are ongoing. We are afraid to talk about God. Some people cannot even bear to sense His presence. The devil undermines our confidence, de-stabilizes us, fills us with doubt and distorts the Truth until we can no longer walk comfortably with God. Satan, as Christ says, came to destroy, he leads us with all the subtlety of the serpent, on the path to destruction. This is our battle.

When we know nothing about prayer, how do we begin?

Awake in the morning and the first thing you do, thank
God for it, even if you don't feel particularly happy about
the day which is to come. 'This day which the Lord has
made, let us rejoice and be grateful in it.' Once you have
done this, give yourself time to realize the truth of what
you are saying and really mean it, perhaps on the level of
deep conviction and not of what one might call exhilara-
tion. And then get up, wash, clean, do whatever else you
have got to do, and then come to God again. Come to
God again with two convictions. The one is that you are
God's own and the other is that this day is also God's
own, it is absolutely new, absolutely fresh. It has never
existed before. To speak in Russian terms, it is like a vast
expanse of unsoiled snow. No one has trodden on it yet.
It is all virgin and pure in front of you. And now, what
comes next? What comes next is that you ask God to bless
this day, that everything in it should be blessed and ruled
by Him ...

... if you accept that this day was blessed of God,
chosen by God with His own hand, then every person you
meet is a gift of God, every circumstance you will meet is
a gift of God, whether it is bitter or sweet, whether you
like or dislike it. It is God's own gift to you and if you take
it that way, then you can face any situation ...

METROPOLITAN ANTHONY OF SOUROZH

School for Prayer

5

Prince Vladimir of Kiev sent emissaries to different countries in order to find a Christian religion for Russia. These emissaries came to the Greeks 'and they led us to the place where their God dwelt', St Sophia in Constantinople. 'We did not know whether we were in Heaven or earth, because nowhere on earth is there such beauty. We only knew that God Himself dwelt there with His people.' And so Orthodoxy came to Russia.

The first Russian Cathedral, Saint Sophia of Novgorod was built in the late 10th century. 'An Orthodox Church represents the duality of existence, its dual form and content foreshadowing through size, geometry and colour the duality of earth and Heaven, body and soul, the human and divine.'

Orthodoxy has been persecuted by atheism, tyrannies and regimes but it has known neither reformation nor counter reformation:

> While the official face of the Church is so often turned towards political activity, it is the hidden depth of the Orthodox Church in its Liturgy and its sacred art which has retained the purity and strength of the Church's apostolic origins.

ARCHIMANDRITE ISAIAS SIMONOPETRITIS

One of the deepest impressions the convert to Orthodoxy receives is that he is in a thing greater than himself, in a Church that knows its own mind because it has remained faithful to the original deposit of the faith. This revelation of one's littleness should make one humble and grateful and willing to learn from those cradles in the faith. We enter a formed Tradition; we do not enter to form – but to be formed; not to teach – but to be taught; not to enlighten – but to be enlightened, and then to transmit this light through a life that is being transformed by the Uncreated Light which shines through the liturgical life of the Church. This is the convert's pilgrimage –

ARCHIMANDRITE BARNABAS

O Lord, grant me to greet the coming day in peace. Help me in all things to rely upon thy holy will. Bless my dealings with all who surround me. Teach me to treat all that comes to me throughout the day with peace of soul, and with firm conviction that thy will governs all. In all my deeds and words guide my thoughts and feelings. In unforeseen events let me not forget that all are sent by thee. Teach me to act firmly and wisely, without embittering and embarrassing others. Give me strength to bear the fatigue of the coming day with all that it shall bring. Direct my will, teach me to pray, pray thou thyself in me. Amen.

METROPOLITAN PHILARET OF MOSCOW (D. 1867)

Prayer at the Beginning of the Day

I am the Way, the Truth and the Life (John 14.6)

Without God's grace we *can* do nothing; but without our voluntary co-operation God *will* do nothing.

THE HOMILY OF ST MACARIUS

The Fathers take the two Old Testament figures of Abraham and Moses as symbols of the spiritual Way. Abraham is simply commanded to 'Go out ...' (Genesis 12.1) Moses has three visions (Exod 3.2; 13.21; 20.21).

Abraham journeys from his familiar home into an unknown country; Moses progresses from light into darkness. And so it proves to be for each one who follows the spiritual Way. We go out from the known into the unknown, we advance from light into darkness. We do not simply proceed from the darkness of ignorance into the light of knowledge, but we go forward from the light of partial knowledge into a greater knowledge which is so much more profound that it can only be described as the 'darkness of unknowing'.

BISHOP KALLISTOS OF DIOKLEIA

The Orthodox Way

We in the modern world have a great deal of the lower kinds of knowledge: factual, practical, scientific, philosophical, theological. But the highest knowledge, the only one capable of touching God, is very rare. Few people know what it is like, some would doubt its possibility, many would deny it outright. The lower forms of knowledge, which are so familiar to us, are not merely incapable of reaching God, they actually blot him out, prevent the knowledge of him from dawning in our minds. This is because they work upon the senses, and upon information derived from the senses.

When sense-impressions, images and ideas have been cast aside, then the knowledge of God can shine forth ... it is direct, immediate, intuitive. Knower and known are united in an instantaneous flash of illumination; nothing is allowed to intervene or mediate between them.

High knowledge is a gift from God, which he is free to give or withhold as he wills. But the fact is that he wants to bestow it on us; he is constantly watching and waiting for his chance to give it to us. The only thing that prevents him is our unwillingness and unreadiness to receive. Once we are ready, God will act immediately, and rush in to flood our whole being with his glory and power.

The goal of Divine Knowledge, then, is high; but not unattainable. We shall attain it, if we truly desire it, even though everything depends upon that 'if'.

CYPRIAN SMITH

The Way of Paradox

 9

A meditation

God has created me to do Him some definite service. He has committed some work to me which He has not committed to another. I have my mission – I may never know it in this life, but I shall be told it in the next.

I am a link in a chain, a bond of connection between persons. He has not created me for naught. I shall do good. I shall do His work. I shall be an angel of peace, a preacher of truth in my own place while not intending it – if I do but keep His commandments.

Therefore I will trust Him. Whatever, wherever I am. I can never be thrown away. If I am in sickness, my sickness may serve Him, in perplexity, my perplexity may serve Him, if I am in sorrow my sorrow may serve Him. He does nothing in vain. He knows what He is about. He may take away my friends. He may throw me among strangers. He may make me feel desolate, make my spirit sink, hide my future from me – still He knows what He is about.

CARDINAL NEWMAN

Send out thy light and thy truth
 let them lead me,
let them bring me to thy holy hill
 and to thy dwelling.

(PSALM 43.3)

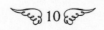

O Heavenly King, O Comforter, the Spirit of truth, who art everywhere and fillest all things, the treasure of blessings, and giver of life, come and abide in us. Cleanse us from all impurity, and of thy goodness save our souls.

PRAYER TO THE HOLY SPIRIT

Eastern Orthodox Church

While we are being strengthened in Christ Jesus and beginning to move forward in steadfast watchfulness, He at first appears in our intellect like a torch which, carried in the hand of the intellect, guides us along the tracks of the mind; then He appears like a full moon, circling the heart's firmament; then He appears to us like the sun, radiating justice, clearly revealing Himself in the full light of spiritual vision.

ST HESYCHIOS THE PRIEST

The Philokalia, Volume I

Watchfulness means, among other things, to be present where we are – at this specific point in space, at this particular moment in time. All too often we are scattered and dispersed, we are living, not with alertness in the present, but with nostalgia in the past, or with misgiving and wishful thinking in the future. While we are indeed required responsibly to plan for the future – for watchfulness is the opposite of fecklessness – we are to think about the future only so far as it depends upon the present moment. Anxiety over remote possibilities which lie altogether beyond our immediate control is sheer waste of our spiritual energies.

The *neptic* man, then, is gathered into the here and the now. He is the one who seizes the *kairos*, the decisive moment of opportunity.

No contemplation of any kind is possible without *nepsis* or watchfulness. I cannot contemplate either nature or God without learning to be present where I am.

BISHOP KALLISTOS OF DIOKLEIA

The Orthodox Way

Growing in watchfulness and self-knowledge, the traveller upon the Way begins to acquire the power of discrimination or discernment (in Greek, *diakrisis*). This acts as a spiritual sense of taste. Just as the physical sense of taste, if healthy, tells a man at once whether food is mouldy or wholesome, so the spiritual taste, if developed through ascetic effort and prayer, enables a man to distinguish between the varying thoughts and impulses within him. He learns the difference between the evil and the good, between the superfluous and the meaningful, between the fantasies inspired by the devil and the images marked upon his creative imagination by celestial archetypes.

BISHOP KALLISTOS OF DIOKLEIA

The Orthodox Way

It is difficult for a Christian especially in his early years to see where divine providence is leading him. This is because God is most gracious. He leads little by little. 'He does not show you whither He is leading you; you might be frightened did you see the whole prospect at once. ... I can well believe that you have hopes now which you cannot give up, and even which support you in your present course. Be it so: whether they will be fulfilled, or not, is in His hand. He may be pleased to grant the desires of your heart; if so, thank Him for His mercy; only be sure, that all will be for your highest good.' Trust, complete and utter trust, is an essential ingredient in following the Providence of God.

VINCENT FERRER BLEHL, SJ

The White Stone

Teach me the way I should go ...
Teach me to do thy will
    for thou art my God.
Let thy good spirit lead me
    on a level path.

(PSALM 143.8.10)

Encounter at the Well

Now Jacob's well was there. Jesus therefore, being wearied with his journey, sat thus on the well: and it was about the sixth hour.

(John 4.5)

Maybe some believers, who consider themselves 'enlightened' and 'reasonable' (but whose view of the history of salvation is very superficial), would shrug their shoulders if they were told that it is not a matter of indifference for a faithful Christian, whether on a certain day he writes one letter rather than another, or goes by bus rather than underground. Admittedly God leaves us free to make choices according to our own lights, nevertheless he has, in relation to everything, a thought, a wish, for which certain definite means are appropriate. It is always open to us, without any childishness or superstition, but humbly and with confidence, to consult God on every single matter (this practice is, in effect, the total essential obedience of the monk). We must let ourselves be guided to Jacob's Well to meet the woman of Samaria. We must accept a guided life in order to discover, in our own life and in the lives of others, the numberless cases of 'he must needs go through Samaria' which we have not sought for or anticipated, but by means of which God is weaving the pattern of our destiny.

Father Lev Gillett

Extract from a retreat address

 15

Move not, speak not – look to the pillar of the cloud. See how it moves, then follow.

CARDINAL NEWMAN

God knows what is my greatest happiness, but I do not. There is no rule about what is happy and good, what suits one would not suit another. And the ways by which perfection is reached vary very much, the medicines necessary for our souls are very different from each other. Thus God leads us by strange ways, we know He wills our happiness, but we neither know what our happiness is, nor the way. We are blind, left to ourselves we should take the wrong way, we must leave it to Him.

CARDINAL NEWMAN

O Lord, deprive me not of thy heavenly blessings.

O Lord, if I have sinned in mind or thought, in word or deed, forgive me.

O Lord, deliver me from every ignorance and heedlessness, from littleness of soul and stony hardness of heart.

O Lord, deliver me from every temptation.

O Lord, send down thy grace to help me, that I may glorify thy Holy Name.

O Lord Jesus Christ, enrol me, thy servant, in the book of life, and grant me a blessed end.

O Lord my God, even if I have done nothing good in thy sight, yet grant me, according to thy grace, to make a beginning of good.

O Lord, sprinkle on my heart the dew of thy grace.

O Lord, of heaven and earth, remember me, thy sinful servant, cold of heart and impure, in thy Kingdom.

ST JOHN CHRYSOSTOM

People who do not know God, or who go against Him, are to be pitied: the heart sorrows for them and the eye weeps. Both paradise and torment are clearly visible to us: we know them through the Holy Spirit. And did not the Lord Himself say: 'The Kingdom of God is within you?' Thus eternal life has its beginnings here in this life, and here it is that we sow the seeds of eternal torment.

ARCHIMANDRITE SOPHRONY

Wisdom from Mount Athos

O Lord, receive me in repentance.
O Lord, leave me not.
O Lord, lead me not into temptation.
O Lord grant me thought of good.
O Lord, grant me tears, a remembrance of death, and a sense of peace.
O Lord grant me mindfulness to confess my sins.
O Lord, grant me humility, charity, and obedience.
O Lord, grant me endurance, magnanimity, and gentleness.
O Lord, plant in me the root of all blessings, the fear of thee in my heart.
O Lord, vouchsafe that I may love thee with all my heart and soul and in all things obey thy will.
O Lord, shield me from evil men and devils and passions and all other unlawful things.
O Lord, who knowest thy creation and what thou has willed for it; may thy will also be fulfilled in me a sinner; for thou art blessed for evermore. Amen.

ST JOHN CHRYSOSTOM

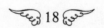

In the early centuries of the church the word 'faith' had already acquired two different meanings, and these represent these two different stages in its growth in the individual. The first of these, the faith that can become knowledge, is more than purely intellectual conviction. The Fathers said that this first form of faith was gained by hearing, which could support the idea that faith of conviction is very little different from blind belief. But experience shows that it is gained not by hearing unsupported doctrine but by the recognition that occurs when a clear statement evokes a particular kind of memory that we were previously unable to articulate adequately. The memories that give rise to this first faith are recollections based on one or more glimpses that were not long enough or not intense enough that we can clearly describe them, even to ourselves. When the nous* recognizes that about which it is hearing, engagement of the heart occurs, and at this exact moment the character of belief changes and faith of conviction comes into being. Since this conviction comes not from any argument but from a memory that is often subconscious, this faith is not blind, yet, as Saint Paul puts it, it still sees as if 'through a glass, darkly.'

ROBIN AMIS

*nous – spiritual intellect

Do not be yoked together with unbelievers ... What does a believer have in common with an unbeliever? ... For we are the temple of the living God. As God has said: 'I will live with them and walk among them, and I will be their God and they will be my people.' Therefore come out from them and be separate, says the Lord. ... And I will receive you. I will be a Father to you, and you will be my sons and daughters, says the Lord Almighty.

(2 Corinthians 6.14–18)

The sincere Christian accepts as a fundamental principle that he has been created by God and that his true happiness consists in serving Him in this life and being conjoined with Him for eternity. To serve God in this life a man must become holy. Moreover, there is a nexus between entering into eternal life and holiness, for 'supposing a man of unholy life were suffered to enter heaven, *he would not be happy there*. 'He must first become holy as God is holy.'

Vincent Ferrer Blehl, sj

The White Stone

Most of us go through life praying a little, planning a little, jockeying for position, hoping but never being quite certain of anything, and always secretly afraid that we will miss the way. This is a tragic waste of truth and never gives rest to the heart.

There is a better way. It is to repudiate our own wisdom and take instead the infinite wisdom of God. Our insistence on seeing ahead is natural enough, but it is a real hindrance to our spiritual progress. God has charged Himself with full responsibility for our eternal happiness and stands ready to take over the management of our lives the moment we turn in faith to Him. Here is His promise:

> And I will bring the blind by a way that they knew not; I will lead them in paths that they have not known; I will make darkness light before them, and crooked things straight. These things will I do unto them, and not forsake them. (Isaiah 42.16 Authorised Version)

A.W. TOZER
Knowledge of the Holy

In order that you may move your will more easily to this one desire in everything – to please God and to work for His glory alone – remind yourself often, that He has granted you many favours in the past and has shown you His love. He has created you out of nothing in His own likeness and image, and has made all other creatures your servants; He has delivered you from your slavery to the devil, sending down not one of the angels but His Only begotten Son to redeem you, not at the price of corruptible gold and silver, but by His priceless blood and His most painful and degrading death. Having done all this He protects you, every hour and every moment, from your enemies; He fights your battles by His divine grace; in His immaculate Mysteries He prepares the Body and Blood of His beloved Son for your food and protection.

NICODEMUS OF THE HOLY MOUNTAIN

Unseen Warfare

... We should feel with our whole heart that we have no one to rely on except God, and that from Him and Him alone can we expect every kind of good, every manner of help, and victory. Since we are nothing, we can expect nothing from ourselves, except stumblings and falls, which make us relinquish all hope of ourselves. On the other hand, we are certain always to be granted victory by God, if we arm our heart with a living trust in Him and an unshakable certainty that we will receive His help, according to the psalm: 'My heart trusted in Him, and I am helped.' (Psalm 28.7)

NICODEMUS OF THE HOLY MOUNTAIN

Unseen Warfare

You must know that progress on the path of spiritual life differs greatly from an ordinary journey on earth. If a traveller stops on his ordinary journey, he loses nothing of the way already covered; but if a traveller on the path of virtue stops in his spiritual progress, he loses much of the virtues previously acquired ... In an ordinary journey, the further the traveller proceeds, the more tired he becomes, but on the way of spiritual life the longer a man travels, ... the greater the strength and power he acquires for his further progress.

NICODEMUS OF THE HOLY MOUNTAIN

Unseen Warfare

Still Waters

'He leadeth me.' In the East there are seldom any well-marked paths. The shepherd has to go ahead of his flock to show the way as well as defend the flock against possible attacks by wild animals.

The Shepherd does not lead his sheep towards just any kind of water. The psalmist speaks of 'still waters'. Why 'still'. Sheep have a great dislike for any water that is agitated or turbulent; they will not drink from torrents, waterfalls or fast-running rivers. They need calm waters, those which are more or less still and unruffled (this is why shepherds often prefer to draw some water and give it to the sheep in suitable vessels). Here there is a profound symbolism. If a sheep is not able to drink quietly, then the water in question has not been given to it by the shepherd, and the animal is wilfully following a useless caprice. The water which the Shepherd gives is never disturbed. It is offered, given without stint, and absorbed slowly, gently. I cannot draw near to the water provided by the Shepherd unless my soul is first of all at peace.

FATHER LEV GILLETT

Encounter at the Well

There are times when we do not need any words of prayer, neither our own nor anyone else's and then we pray in perfect silence. This perfect silence is the ideal prayer, provided, however, that the silence is real and not daydreaming. We have very little experience of what deep silence of body and soul means, when complete serenity fills the soul, when complete peace fills the body, when there is no turmoil or stirring of any sort and when we stand before God, completely open in an act of adoration.

The Greek Fathers set this silence, which they called *hesychia*, both as the starting-point and the final achievement of a life of prayer. Silence is the state in which all the powers of the soul and all the faculties of the body are completely at peace, quiet and recollected, perfectly alert yet free from any turmoil and agitation. A simile which we find in many writings of the Fathers is that of the waters of a pond. As long as there are ripples on the surface, nothing can be reflected properly, neither the trees nor the sky; when the surface is quite still, the sky is perfectly reflected, the trees on the bank and everything is there as distinct as in reality.

METROPOLITAN ANTHONY OF SOUROZH

Living Prayer

Another simile of the same sort used by the Fathers is that as long as the mud which is at the bottom of a pond has not settled, the water is not clear and one can see nothing through it. These two analogies apply to the state of the human heart. 'Blessed are the pure in heart for they shall see God.' (Matthew 5.8) As long as the mud is in motion in the water there is no clear vision through it, and again as long as the surface is covered with ripples there can be no adequate reflection on what surrounds the pond.

As long as the soul is not still there can be no vision, but when stillness has brought us into the presence of God, then another sort of silence, much more absolute, intervenes; the silence of a soul that is not only still and recollected but which is overawed in an act of worship by God's presence; a silence in which, as Julian of Norwich puts it, 'Prayer oneth the soul to God.'

METROPOLITAN ANTHONY OF SOUROZH

Living Prayer

The Miraculous Draught of Fishes

... we consider just what is involved in fishing with a stationary net, which is what the Apostles were doing. This style of fishing involves simply letting down your net, spreading it out a bit and waiting. There is really nothing more you *can* do. You must prepare properly; you must see that your net does not have holes in it: you must use your skill and experience to choose the place where you will fish and manoeuvre your boat there without scaring off your prey. You should let down your net gently. But once the net is in place, you can do little more than wait: whether the fish swim into the net and are caught there is not up to you. Another power is involved.

... It is not only that we, too, can often say with the disciples: 'Master, we have toiled all the night, and have taken nothing.' The Gospel also says to us what Christ says to the disciples: 'Do what I tell you to do, and I will take care of the rest.'

BISHOP BASIL OF SERIEVO

on Luke 5:1–11

'Lord Jesus Christ, Son of God, have mercy on me, a sinner.' This is the most treasured Orthodox prayer from *The Way of The Pilgrim* which is the story of a man who wanted to learn to pray constantly. (1 Thess. 5.1) The prayer is profoundly rooted in the Spirit of the Gospel. The modern translation of the words 'have mercy' are perhaps, limited. Metropolitan Anthony explains:

The Greek word which we find in the gospel and in the early liturgies is *eleison*. *Eleison* is of the same root as *elaion*, which means olive tree and the oil from it. If we look up the Old and New Testament in search of the passages connected with this basic idea, we will find it described in a variety of parables and events which allow us to form a complete idea of the meaning of the word. We find the image of the olive tree in Genesis. After the flood Noah sends birds, one after the other, to find out whether there is any dry land or not, and one of them, a dove — and it is significant that it is a dove — brings back a small twig of olive. The twig conveys to Noah and to all with him in the ark the news that the wrath of God has eased, that God is now offering man a fresh opportunity. All those who are in the ark will be able to settle again on firm ground and make an attempt to live, and never more perhaps, if they can help it, undergo the wrath of God.

METROPOLITAN ANTHONY OF SOUROZH

Living Prayer

In the New Testament, in the parable of the good Samaritan, olive oil is poured to soothe and to heal. In the anointing of kings and priests in the Old Testament, it is again oil that is poured on the head as an image of the grace of God that comes down and flows on them (Psalm 133.2) giving them new power to fulfil what is beyond human capabilities. The king is to stand on the threshold, between the will of men and the will of God, and he is called to lead his people to the fulfilment of God's will; the priest also stands on that threshold to proclaim the will of God and to do even more; to act for God, to pronounce God's decrees and to apply God's decision.

The oil speaks first of all of the end of the wrath of God, of the peace which God offers to the people who have offended against him; further it speaks of God healing us in order that we should be able to live and become what we are called to be.

METROPOLITAN ANTHONY OF SOUROZH

Living Prayer

The words *milost* and *pomiluy* in Slavonic have the same root as those which express tenderness, endearing, and when we use the word *eleison*, 'have mercy on us', we are not just asking God to save us from his wrath – we are asking for love.

If we turn back to the words of the Jesus Prayer, 'Lord Jesus Christ, Son of God, have mercy on me, a sinner', we see that the first words express with exactness and integrity the gospel; faith in Christ, the historical incarnation of the Word of God; and the end of the prayer expresses all the complex rich relationships of love that exist between God and his creatures.

METROPOLITAN ANTHONY OF SOUROZH

Living Prayer

As long as we are ignorant, nothing is asked of us, but as soon as we know anything, we are answerable for the use we make of the knowledge.

METROPOLITAN ANTHONY OF SOUROZH

I trust thee and commit into thy hands my soul and body, my whole life . . .

METROPOLITAN ANTHONY OF SOUROZH

Living Prayer

. . . having once given your life and your will to God as a reasonable offering, EVERYTHING that happens to you is sanctioned by Him because he allows only such things to happen to you, when once you have put your life in His hands, as can do you some good. Nine times out of ten you will be able to see. The tenth perhaps you won't. Just make a note of it and ask God to show you.

The quantity of a man's sinfulness varies with his opportunities and his will-power. Some people never have the chance of sinning. Some inherit a will which makes sin simply loathsome. On the other hand, some contract the habit of sinning in ignorance, and inherit such a damaged will that they cannot break the habit.

It is now or never. While we live we must make up our minds — whether we shall please ourselves and enjoy this life in our own way, or whether we shall take only what joy God gives us in doing His will and live with Christ in Eternity.

We have to choose!

FROM THE DIARIES OF EDWARD WILSON OF THE ANTARCTIC
who accompanied Scott and Shackleton
to the South Pole in 1910

 31

There are certain priorities in prayer which the liturgical services alone can teach us – God's Presence, aweful yet homely, the need in us to give Him the praise and thanks which He deserves, the positive presence of the Angels and Saints which assures us of the existence of our 'long home' (Ecclesiastes 12.5) towards which we are travelling.

We need faith to enter fully into this Mystery, but if our faith wanes it is nourished by worship ... Worship strengthens our moral fibre and gives us insights as it did to the Psalmist 'Then thought I to understand this, but it was too hard for me, until I went into the sanctuary of God.' (Psalm 73.16)

FATHER BARNABAS

O Almighty Lord, Word of the Father, Jesus Christ, who art thyself perfect, for thy great mercy's sake do thou never depart from me, thy servant, but ever abide in me. O Jesus, Good Shepherd of thy sheep let me not fall into the disobedience of the serpent nor leave me to the will of Satan, for the seed of corruption is in me. Do thou, therefore, O Lord God whom we worship, O Holy King Jesus, preserve me while I sleep with thy unchanging light, thy Holy Spirit, wherewith thou didst sanctify thy disciples. Grant, O Lord, even to me, thy unworthy servant, thy salvation upon my bed; enlighten my mind with the light of the understanding of thy holy Gospel, my soul with the love of thy Cross, my heart with the purity of thy Word, my body with thy passionless passion; preserve my thought in thy humility and rouse me at the fit time to glorify thee. For thou art glorified above all, with thy Eternal Father and with the most Holy Spirit for evermore. Amen.

ST ANTIOKH

Evening Prayer

The Word

In the beginning was the Word,
and the Word was with God,
and the Word was God.

(JOHN 1.1)

The Words that I have spoken to you
are spirit and life.

(JOHN 6.63)

The Words that I have spoken to you are spirit and life.
(John 6.61)

Those wonderful words of Christ made no sense to me until I discovered the Orthodox way of presenting Christianity. God speaks to us through His Word and yet for many people in the West these words have sadly never come to life. The parables are still mixed up with the Maths results in School Assembly, read by the wrong person with the wrong emphasis, and no idea of God. Leaving us too often with a memory of admonishment and of blame, rather than Wisdom and Love.

It wasn't until I discovered the Orthodox way of presenting Christianity that everything changed. The Book of the Gospels in the Orthodox Church is brought out from the Sanctuary (which represents Heaven) into the body of the Church (which represents Earth). The word Wisdom is chanted by the Deacon to emphasise its importance and the Gospel is held high in reverence, covering the face of the priest who carries it. Suddenly, for me, the Word became Flesh. It was no longer merely a concept.

The rather flat way of reading the Scriptures in Orthodoxy is no accident. It removes human emphasis and so one mysteriously discovers God's emphasis perhaps for the first time. Again The Word is God's Word and does not belong to the reader who acts out his own interpretation.

Why is it that for so many of us in this country The Word hasn't 'come to life?' Even if we think we know the Bible, how many can truthfully say:

> Did not our hearts burn within us while he talked to us on the road, while he opened to us the Scriptures.
>
> (Luke 24.32)

That is not a moderate or mild reaction. There is something ecstatic about it. It has taken me nearly a lifetime to understand the intensity of those words.

I was born in Malaya. My mother died when I was a year old and I was sent home and brought up by my mother's sister and her husband in a small village on the west coast of Scotland. My father, who was a rubber planter, remained in Malaya and was subsequently taken prisoner of war by the Japanese. My uncle was a Presbyterian minister. We lived in a large, bleak manse with three pianos, an organ, a bottled tarantula, porridge, twenty hens, and a black engine which generated our own electricity. The house was very cold and icicles hung from the ceilings like crystal chandeliers. The grey black colours of the manse seemed to symbolize my faith.

My uncle's study was dark. Papers and sermons lay on the floor in disarray, and the desk was piled with rusty pennies, bottled scorpions, dried lizards, prune stones, and homemade treacle toffee that looked like black broken glass. The darkness has stayed in my memory, as though a seed had to be broken in the darkness before it could reach the light. My uncle loved thick pimply porridge that he insisted on cooking himself on a primus stove, which sent volcanic flames three feet into the air. As for religion, perhaps it was not surprising that I cannot remember the Gospels. I remember only the Old Testament, but out of context and incomplete. The plague of locusts, the plagues of darkness, and burning in the lowest Hell. 'The sword without, the terror within shall destroy both the young man and the virgin, the suckling also with the man of grey hairs.' 'And Moses stretched his hand towards heaven, and there was thick darkness in all the land of Egypt, and for three days they saw not one another.'

As an exercise I have often tried to re-enter this period of my life with the knowledge that I have now and not with the limited vision of childhood. But this is like forcing a piece of jigsaw puzzle into the wrong place.

Every Sunday I sat in the front pew of the church on a prickly horse hair cushion. I listened to my uncle's sermons all through childhood and never heard a word.

Much later, I married into the Establishment, into an environment which was Anglican rather than Presbyterian. God was now like a Patron's name on a letter heading. You knew He was important but nobody had introduced you. Religion for us in the 1960s was an accepted rather formal obligation on a social and national level; something external. We sat up straight in the crested pew of our village church. We sang hymns lustily and listened to the weekly sermon. Private prayer consisted of lowering your head among the hymn books and usually making a hurried list of superficial requests: a self-conscious moment before the service began. I don't think that one was expected to pray deeply. People would have stared in astonishment. There was no mystery, no stillness; the natural environment through which God can act. Inspiration depended on the eloquence of the sermon or the loudness of the hymn singing. Sometimes a seed was sown but it seldom germinated.

I never sensed that I was in the undiluted awesome holiness of His presence: a feeling I was later to experience in the Orthodox Church.

I believe that God sometimes lets us out on a very long thread, rather like Ariadne who guided Theseus through the labyrinth. But how wonderful when He pulls us back to where we are meant to be. The Word then takes on a completely different quality and begins to move us in the same way that it moved the two Apostles on their walk to Emmaus.

Now that I am Orthodox I have a small Chapel. It was once an ice house and then used for coal and rubbish. It is surprisingly beautiful for such a humble place, mediaeval, vaulted and with limestone arches. It is now filled with icons and candlelight and used only for prayer. It is easy to feel God's presence in such a place. Perhaps it was from here that The Word moved into the next stage of understanding.

God speaks to us through the Scriptures. Sometimes another human being has to ignite our interest and knowledge. Then we can forget the memories of voices from the past which may have held no meaning for us.

We can simply say some of His Words every day, deeply, like a prayer. These will vary as we discover more words.

I am the vine you are the branches, He who abides in me, and I in him, he it is that bears much fruit, for apart from me you can do nothing. (JOHN 15.5)

As the Father has loved me, so have I loved you, abide in my love. (JOHN 15.9)

If a man loves me he will keep my word, and my Father will love him, and we will come to him and make our home with him. (JOHN 14.23)

Behold I stand at the door and knock, if any one hears my voice and opens the door, I will come in to him and eat with him, and he with me. (REVELATION E.20)

Do not be anxious about tomorrow, for tomorrow will be anxious for itself. Let the day's own trouble be sufficient for the day. (MATTHEW 6.34)

Then there are the priorities:

Seek first His Kingdom and his righteousness and all these things will be yours as well. (MATTHEW 6.25–34)

My grace is sufficient for you. (2 COR.12.9)

This is God speaking directly to us.

There are beautiful, hidden words in Isaiah:

I will give you the treasures of darkness and the hoards in secret places that you may know that it is I, the Lord, the God of Israel, who calls you by your name.

(ISAIAH 45.3)

Finally we can explore the Psalms. There are some powerful verses that might seem discordant and anguished, but in times of distress these emotions have always been the same. The Psalmist puts them into words and prayers for us:

Save me, O God!
For the waters have come up to my neck,
I sink in deep mire, where there is no foothold;
I have come into deep waters, and the flood sweeps over me,
I am weary with my crying; my throat is parched,
My eyes grow dim with waiting for my God . . .
Insults have broken my heart so that I am in despair,
I looked for pity but there was none; and for comforters,
but I found none . . . (FROM PSALM 69)

I know, O Lord, that thy judgements are right, and that in faithfulness thou has afflicted me.
Let thy steadfast love be ready to comfort me according to thy promise to thy servant. Let thy mercy come to me, that I may live; for thy law is my delight.

Blessed be thou, O Lord, teach me thy statutes.

Keep steady my steps according to thy promise, and let no iniquity get dominion over me. Redeem me from man's oppression, that I may keep thy precepts. Make thy face shine upon thy servant, and teach me thy statutes.

Let my cry come before thee, O Lord, give me understanding according to thy word! . . . My lips will pour forth praise that thou dost teach me thy statutes. My tongue will sing of thy words for all thy commandments are right. Let thy hand be ready to help me, for I have chosen thy precepts.

Blessed be thou, O Lord, teach me thy statutes.

(FROM PSALM 119)

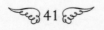 41

The Psalms, repeated so often in their entirety throughout the Liturgy and throughout the Hours in the Orthodox Church, become a familiar way of worship and an intimate living prayer. It is a continual dialogue with God:

Teach me thy way, O Lord, and I will walk in thy truth:
O knit my heart unto thee, that I may fear thy Name.

FROM PSALM 86

Ninth Hour

... thou requirest truth, in the inward parts, and shall make me to understand wisdom secretly. Thou shalt purge me with hyssop, and I shall be clean: thou shalt wash me, and I shall be whiter than snow. Thou shalt make me hear of joy and gladness, that the bones which thou has broken may rejoice. Turn thy face from my sins, and put out all my misdeeds. Make me a clean heart, O God, and renew a right spirit within me. Cast me not away from thy presence, and take not thy Holy Spirit from me.

FROM PSALM 51

Third Hour

O how amiable are thy dwellings, thou Lord of hosts! My soul hath a desire and longing to enter into the courts of the Lord: my heart and my flesh rejoice in the living God. Yea, the sparrow hath found her an house, and the swallow a nest, where she may lay her young; even at thy altars O Lord of hosts, my King and my God. Blessed are they that dwell in thy house; they will be always praising thee. Blessed is the man whose strength is in thee in whose heart are thy ways. Who going through the vale of misery use it for a well; and the pools are filled with water. They will go from strength to strength ... For one day in thy courts is better than a thousand. I had rather be a door keeper in the house of my God, than to dwell in the tents of ungodliness. For the Lord God is a light and defence ... O Lord God of hosts, blessed is the man that putteth his trust in thee.

FROM PSALM 84

Ninth Hour

I will lift up mine eyes unto the hills, from whence cometh my help. My help cometh even from the Lord, who hath made heaven and earth. He will not suffer thy foot to be moved, and he that keepeth Israel shall neither slumber nor sleep. The Lord himself is thy keeper: the Lord is thy defence upon thy right hand so that the sun shall not burn thee by day, neither the moon by night. The Lord shall preserve thee from all evil: yea, it is even he that shall keep thy soul. The Lord shall preserve thy going out and thy coming in, from this time forth, even forevermore.

Glory to the Father, and to the Son, and to the Holy Spirit, now, and ever, and unto ages of ages. Amen.

PSALM 121
Used by the Orthodox Church in the Rite of Blessing
those who are about to travel by water

The Storm Stilled

The storm is on the surface. We are told not to look at the size of the waves that threaten to engulf us, or to measure the depth of the sea ... Be still and know that God is with you.

One day he got into a boat with his disciples, and he said to them, 'Let us go across to the other side of the lake.' So they set out, and as they sailed he fell asleep. And a storm of wind came down on the lake, and they were filling with water, and were in danger. And they went and woke him, saying, 'Master, Master, we are perishing!' And he awoke and rebuked the wind and the raging waves; and they ceased, and there was a calm. He said to them 'Where is your faith?' And they were afraid, and they marvelled, saying to one another, 'Who then is this, that he commands even wind and water, and they obey him?'

LUKE 8.22–25

45

If it had not been the Lord who was on our side,
when men rose up against us,
then they would have swallowed us up alive
then their anger was kindled against us;
when the flood would have swept us away,
the torrent would have gone over us,
then over us would have gone the raging waters.
Blessed be the Lord, who has not given us as prey to their
   teeth.
We have escaped as a bird from the snare of the fowlers,
the snare is broken and we have escaped!
Our help is in the name of the Lord who made heaven and
   earth.

(Psalm 124)

How graphic is Psalm 124, one of the Songs of Ascent. Of David. It has
been called 'The Psalm of the Broken Snare.'

Thanksgiving for God's deliverance

You are trapped in a perilous situation like a bird in a
snare. There is no way out. The future is grim. Then
suddenly, unaccountably, the snare breaks and you are
free! A miracle has happened ... life on this planet is
hazardous. We have no idea what will happen to us in
the hours that lie ahead. Before this day is over we may
have to deal with such matters as serious illness, a
domestic crisis, physical or emotional pain, death, a
financial reverse, a broken relationship, redundancy,
rejection, perhaps even a national or world emergency.
We live from one day to the next on the edge of danger,
and sometimes we become caught up in situations from
which there seems just no way out. Then God comes in
glorious deliverance. The trap is broken and our soul is
set free.

That doesn't always happen as quickly as we would like, and it doesn't always happen the way we would like; it happens in the way that God sees best. He steps in, releases the snare and our soul soars, like a bird set free.

SELWYN HUGHES

Every Day with Jesus

So Jeremiah ... stayed ... among the people who were left behind in the land.

(JEREMIAH 40.6)

This is a wonderful moment in Jeremiah's life. It takes place after the fall of Jerusalem. The prophet can go to Babylon where he will be given special treatment – no chains, no imprisonment, no deprivation. Or he can return to Jerusalem, a city now in ruins, and be part of the tiny remnant left behind ... He chose to return to Jerusalem and live as he had always lived, trusting God and confident in His purposes. Jeremiah's choice that day was typical of how he had lived all his life. He chose to be where the Almighty had enshrined His Name – Jerusalem, the city of God. Comfort or service? The choice faces us daily, not just at life's big crossroads.

Father, I face many choices in life and sometimes attractive choices. But no matter what choices I am faced with help me always to make the choice that is in line with Yours. In Jesus' Name I pray. Amen.

SELWYN HUGHES

Every Day with Jesus

The Lord is my shepherd. I shall not want. He makes me lie down in green pastures. He leads me beside still waters, he restores my soul. He leads me in paths of righteousness, for his name's sake. Even though I walk through the valley of the shadow of death, I fear no evil; for thou art with me, thy rod and thy staff they comfort me.

Thou preparest a table before me in the presence of my enemies; thou anointest my head with oil, my cup overflows. Surely goodness and mercy shall follow me all the days of my life; and I shall dwell in the house of the Lord for ever.

(PSALM 23)

Blessed is our God always, now, and ever, and unto ages of ages. Amen

Spiritual Struggle

Take away the dross from the silver,
and the smith has material for a vessel.

(PROVERBS 24.4)

The Heart of the pilgrim is the battleground on which the battle is fought.

ARCHIMANDRITE BARNABAS

On the Other Side of the Cross

A young builder moved the iron cross on the front of our house from being a kiss-shaped cross to a Christ-shaped Cross. It supported a heavy beam and was on the outside wall of my bedroom at the exact spot where I prayed. I didn't ask him to do it. He just felt it might please me. He wasn't a fervent Christian by any means but he had courtesy and the capacity to understand.

'You are on the other side of the cross,' observed a hermit friend.

At that stage I didn't know what it meant. I imagined that the Cross would be a comfortable kind of protection – life would be plain sailing without problems ... I didn't realize the full implication of these words.

As we move along our path on the pilgrimage to Christ we continually learn lessons; the lessons become more difficult and each one must bring us closer to Him. If we are not on the path to Christ there are no fruits borne of our suffering but it seems that if we are serious, we may have to face and share in at least some aspects of His Passion before we can proceed. Most Christian mystics and visionaries are made to feel and experience the events that led to Calvary with great intensity before they are able to understand or to receive further revelation. It is a classic religious situation, which would make the dark and bewildering periods of our lives much more acceptable and meaningful if we were taught to recognize it. It may be physical pain and cruelty that we experience; Christ was scourged and beaten and kicked. It may be a broken spirit, mockery of our faith, and angry abuse, as He experienced. It may be hatred, humiliation and callousness; being blamed unjustly; it may be homelessness, our material security taken away from us, and that those whom we love most betray us. All these things were experienced by Christ, they are the ongoing wounds of Christ, and if we share in any one of them then we begin to understand the full implication of His Death for us on the Cross. What is meant by living 'on the other side of the Cross.'

I have noticed more than once that after a period of despair and discouragement there has followed a time of grace when God seems closer than ever before, and when His Blessings pour into the new situation. We are taught by means of contrast, and these contrasts illuminate God's love for us. We are not given knowledge of what is going to happen in the future because such knowledge might make it impossible for us to endure what is taking place in the present. In the Old Testament we read of different kinds of testing in order to affirm loyalty to God. There were floods, plagues, famines – today it is perhaps more subtle, but just as real. We walk in the dark and have to live through it, clinging to our growing, battered faith, until like Christ Himself we share not only in His Death, but in His Resurrection.

> The fruits of the inner man begin only with the shedding of tears.

> Where there is no sorrow there is no salvation.

St Seraphim of Sarov

Blessed art thou, O Lord, teach me thy statutes.

Archimandrite Barnabas was a much loved monk in the Orthodox Church. I shall never forget a winter evening with him in the library of our house. He left the shutters wide open to the night sky and lit one candle which shone on his gold altar cross. 'A city set on a hill cannot be hid,' was the way he always referred to this house in the country. Apart from the candle we were alone and in almost total darkness as he read, not from his usual Orthodox Ninth Hour, but from the Benedictine Compline. The pathos and solemnity of his Confession was engraved in my memory. To me he was a most Holy man of God.

Since his death and in his memory, I have often used this Benedictine Compline as prayer before going to bed. It takes about ten minutes. The Psalms are an important discipline in all Christian traditions and the verses at the end are comforting as night approaches.

From the Office of Compline

Brethren, be sober, be vigilant, because your adversary the devil goeth about as a roaring lion, seeking whom he may devour, whom resist steadfast in the faith.

We confess to God Almighty, the Father, the Son, and the Holy Ghost, in the sight of the whole company of heaven, that we have sinned exceedingly, in thought, word and deed, through our fault, our own fault, our own most grievous fault. Wherefore we pray God Almighty, the Father, the Son and the Holy Ghost, to have mercy upon us.

Psalm XXXI 1–6 *In Te, Domine, speravi.*

1   In Thee, O Lord, have I put my trust: let me never be put to confusion, deliver me in Thy righteousness.

2   Bow down Thine ear to me: make haste to deliver me.

3   And be Thou my strong rock, and house of defence; that Thou mayst save me.

4   For Thou art my strong rock, and my castle; be Thou also my guide, and lead me for Thy Name's sake.

5   Draw me out of the net that they have laid privily for me; for Thou art my strength.

6   Into Thy hands I commend my spirit; for Thou has redeemed me, O Lord, Thou God of truth.

Psalm XCI *Qui habitat.*

1 Who so dwelleth under the defence of the most High; shall abide under the shadow of the Almighty.

2 I will say unto the Lord, Thou art my hope, and my strong hold; my God, in Him will I trust.

3 For He shall deliver thee from the snare of the hunter; and from the noisome pestilence.

4 He shall defend thee under His wings, and Thou shalt be safe under His feathers; His faithfulness and truth shall be thy shield and buckler.

5 Thou shalt not be afraid for any terror by night; nor for the arrow that flieth by day;

6 For the pestilence that walketh in darkness; not for the sickness that destroyeth in the noon day.

7 A thousand shall fall beside thee, and ten thousand at thy right hand; but it shall not come nigh thee.

8 Yea, with thine eyes shalt thou behold; and see the reward of the ungodly.

9   For Thou, Lord, art my hope; Thou hast set Thine house of defence very high.

10   There shall no evil happen unto thee; neither shall any plague come nigh thy dwelling.

11   For He shall give His angels charge over thee; to keep thee in all thy ways.

12   They shall bear thee in their hands; that thou hurt not thy foot against a stone.

13   Thou shalt go upon the lion and adder – the young lion and the dragon shalt thou tread under thy feet.

14   Because he hath set his love upon Me, therefore will I deliver him; I will set him up, because he hath known my Name.

15   He shall call upon Me, and I will hear him; yea, I am with him in trouble; I will deliver him, and bring him to honour.

16   With long life will I satisfy him; and shew him My salvation.
     Glory be to the Father etc.

Te lucis ante terminum

Before the ending of the day,
Creator of the world, we pray
That Thou with wonted love wouldst keep
Thy watch around us while we sleep.
O let no evil dreams be near,
Nor phantoms of the night appear;
Our ghostly enemy restrain
Lest aught of sin our bodies stain.
Almighty Father hear our cry,
Through Jesus Christ our Lord most high,
Who with the Holy Ghost and Thee
Doth live and reign eternally. Amen.

Thou, O Lord, art in the midst of us, and we are called by
Thy Name; leave us not, O Lord our God.
Into thy hands O Lord I commend my spirit.
Keep me O Lord as the apple of an eye.
Hide me under the shadow of Thy wings.

THE LITTLE CHAPTER

(Jer.XIV 9)

Nunc dimittis

Lord, now lettest Thou Thy servant depart in peace;
according to Thy word.
For mine eyes have seen Thy salvation.
Which Thou has prepared; before the face of all people;
To be a light to lighten the Gentiles; and to be the
glory of Thy people Israel.
Glory be to the Father etc.
As it was in the beginning, etc

Visit, we beseech Thee, O Lord, this dwelling, and drive
far from it all the snares of the enemy. Let Thy holy angels
dwell in it, to preserve us in peace, and may Thy blessing
be upon us evermore; through our Lord Jesus Christ.

Amen.

Look down, O Lord, from Thy heavenly throne, illuminate the darkness of this night with Thy celestial
brightness, and from the sons of light banish the deeds of
darkness; through Jesus Christ our Lord. Amen.

Be present, O merciful God, and protect us through the
silent hours of this night, so that we who are fatigued by
the changes and chances of this fleeting world, may repose
upon Thy eternal changelessness, through Jesus Christ our
Lord. Amen (Ambrosian)

May the Almighty God, the Father, the Son, and the Holy
Ghost, bless, preserve, and keep us, this night, and for
evermore. Amen.

Crisis of Faith

'What I tell you in darkness, speak ye in Light.'

ARCHIMANDRITE BARNABAS

(from Matthew 10.27)

Father Barnabas died on 17th March 1996, before we were able to discuss his contribution to this book. He had led me with encouragement and love through a time when I was seriously trying to move closer to God. He knew the difficulties and dangers and his expressions 'the lions', 'the enemy', 'the Devil', 'evil', were natural to the vocabulary of an Orthodox Hermit and Abbot living and practising the Byzantine Way of Prayer. These words did not refer to other people but to the 'principalities and powers' which are used to discourage and dishearten us. (Ephesians 6.11–12). *Diablos* in Greek means literally 'to tear apart' and if we do not understand our adversary that is what can happen.

Father Barnabas wrote me many letters of spiritual instruction during the last years of his life. I think he hoped I might consider taking monastic vows one day. His letters always started: 'Dear Marina' and their endings varied from 'Votre devoue dans le Seigneur' to 'Your Fellow Pilgrim' A. Barnabas.

Father Barnabas particularly touched on those bleak times when there seems to be an 'absence of God'. (Those periods when, for various reasons and until we are truly confident in our faith, we may *feel* we have lost the closeness and joy that we had at the beginning.)

There seems to be a subtle and quite sudden 'Divide' when our faith moves into a certain stage. Those difficult words of Christ 'I AM THE WAY, THE TRUTH AND THE LIFE' (John 14.6) are full of commitment, as is that other passage 'Seek first His Kingdom, and these things will be yours as well.' Once these words make sense to us we accept them without any further questioning and we are no longer 'part-time' Christians in name only. It has suddenly become our life. Our every moment. We find we have a completely different set of priorities and values and we need all the resources of the Scriptures and of our Tradition behind us. We are no longer interested in purely material things or in the life we once had because we have found something of infinitely higher value. We are passing from 'death to life' (1 John 3.13) and we discover the reality of the 'hatred of the world'. 'Do not be surprised . . . if the world hates you. We know that we have passed from death to life.'

This is a time when private faith is not enough; we need facts and evidence to support it. Two different kinds of knowledge assail us – the human logic: the Laws of the World – and spiritual knowledge: the Laws of God. We may be tempted to renounce our faith, dilute it a little, smudge away the strength of it, and simply rejoin the world. But it is probably too late, God has called us with his love, as in the allegory of the Song of Solomon, the feeling that He has gone from us simply makes us pursue the vision more urgently. And our spiritual struggle begins:

> I sought him but found him not
> I called him but he gave no answer
> I will arise now and go about the city
> in the streets and in the squares
> I will seek him whom my soul loves
> I sought him, but found him not . . .

One feels the urgency in these verses from Chapter 3 in the Song of Solomon. But there is hope in Romans 8.38:

> For I am sure that neither death nor life, nor angels, nor
> principalities, nor things present, nor things to come, nor
> powers, nor height, nor depth, nor anything else that is in
> all creation will be able to separate us from the love of
> God in Christ Jesus our Lord.

How do we survive this first testing of our faith? Father Barnabas compared it to his life as a hermit and wrote as follows:

A Life of Prayer needs a stable setting if a rhythm is to be established, and if you have a high ideal be sure the devil will begin his attacks on you.

When we attempt something beautiful for God it attracts the two opposing forces: the good and the bad. Both forces converge in the heart of the pilgrim and the heart of the pilgrim is the battleground on which the battle is fought. The Russians have a word for it – podvig – and this struggle is referred to again and again in the Philokalia.

We must be striving for beauty, harmony, love, however hard the task may be and anything you can do to counteract the deep sickness in humanity at present – writing, praying, advising, listening, is a blessed work.

Keep your house as a 'city set on a hill which cannot be hid'.

Make it an oasis so that others can feel the presence and love of God always.

Sooner or later we will be severely tested. Immediately after His Baptism when the Heavens opened and He saw the Spirit of God descending like a dove, Christ was led into the Wilderness to be tempted by the Devil. (Matthew 4.1–11)

This is the classic stage that we also go through, often following on closely from a Grace, from a time of great Holiness, as in the case of Christ Himself. The devil tempts using rational argument and Christ answers with the words of the Scriptures for that is the strongest defence when our faith is under threat. Perhaps we are not yet sufficiently familiar with the Scriptures and our attempts will alienate us even further from the world ...

Saturate your surroundings with prayer. Do not be afraid to bathe in the atmosphere (of the Chapel) 'so pure, so clean, so positive.' And as we go into the world to face further trials – know that your little House of God exists and the lamps still burn before the icons, shedding a glory which transforms us ... 'You possess a little Sanctuary for God' (Ezekiel 11.16).

FATHER BARNABAS

But if circumstances change then 'acceptance is one of the hardest words in the spiritual vocabulary.' 'The discipline of disappointment.' 'Some sort of dispassion in the theological sense, is also a state to be reached. It is not easy. Calmness, acceptance, peace are all part of it. Your senses may be disturbed, but you go on with your prayers, though your heart be as lead, and press on through deep darkness until a glimmer of light appears. You may have to learn this doctrine in your life, a very important one in monastic life, and also to lead you to a state when only you and God exist, totally depropped.' Remember we are in His Hands and our prayer must always be 'Not as I will but as Thou Willest.'

Finally, bretheren, whatever is true, whatever is honourable, whatever is just, whatever is pure, whatever is lovely, whatever is gracious, if there is any excellence, if there is anything worthy of praise, think about these things. What you have learned ... do, and the God of peace will be with you.

(PHILLIPPIANS 4.8–9)

FATHER BARNABAS

No Room at the Inn

One can never fully understand the terror of being 'homeless' unless one has experienced it. A 'home' is something we all take for granted – a safe place to sleep quietly, a place where you are loved and protected from the outside world. But there may come an abrupt moment when unaccountably, unexpectedly, everything changes. However temporary, it will still hold the feeling of rejection, helplessness and fear.

This is a passage for all those who at some time in their lives may have to experience this most uncomfortable situation.

> Joseph was full of expectancy as he entered the city of his family, and was quite convinced that he would have no difficulty in finding lodgings for Mary, particularly on account of her condition. Joseph went from house to house only to find each one crowded. He searched in vain for a place where He, to Whom heaven and earth belonged, might be born. Could it be that the Creator would not find a home in creation? Up a steep hill Joseph climbed to a faint light which swung on a rope across a doorway. This would be the village inn. There, above all other places, he would surely find shelter. There was room in the inn for the soldiers of Rome who had brutally subjugated the Jewish people; there was room for those clothed in soft garments, who lived in the houses of the king; in fact, there was room for anyone who had a coin to give the innkeeper; but there was no room for Him Who came to be the Inn of every homeless heart in the world. When finally the scrolls of history are completed down to the last words in time, the saddest line of all will be: 'There was no room in the inn.'

FULTON J. SHEEN
Life of Christ

A poem which I found framed in a guest bedroom in Marigold Bridgeman's house. Its simplicity and comfort spoke to me at a time in my life when I needed this sort of message from a loving God.

Wonder and the Shepherd

Where are you going, Shepherd?
To find my sheep.
How far will you go?
As far as my sheep.
How far may that be?
To the World's end.
How long will you seek it?
Until I find it.
When you find it, will it come to you?
No, it will fly from me.
Where will it go then?
To the rock and the sand.
When will it stop?
When it can run no more.
What will you do then?
Carry it home.

'Lead us not into temptation' – submit us not to the severe test – must remind us of the forty years the Jews spent crossing the short expanse of territory between the land of Egypt and the promised land. They took so long because whenever they turned away from God, their path turned away from the promised land.

METROPOLITAN ANTHONY OF SOUROZH

Living Prayer

 63

Do Not Sin in Your Anger

Be angry but do not sin. Do not let the sun go down on your anger. (Ephes. 4.25)

In the Old Testament we see God's 'divine wrath' many times. He is angered because men break His Laws – because they pay homage to idols. However, if we look closely behind this anger or divine wrath, at its core we can perceive a mysterious arcane force that is the source of everything: Love. For which it is clear the divine anger is the necessary correlative of this divine love, which seeks man's salvation.

In the New Testament Christ is angered at the merchants in the Temple. Defiling the House of God. Again He is angry because of love.

So when we are angry is it a selfish anger, or is it because we are consumed by love for God and our neighbour? Are we capable, as Padre Pio taught his spiritual children, of being angry without sinning?

GERARD DI CUMERI

When there is a spiritual problem do not consult worldly friends who are unable to see beyond the immediate situation. Seek out people of real holiness who understand the eternal value of things. Cultivate such people all through your life for it may one day make the difference between death and life.

As your faith moves closer to God don't be surprised if you feel like an exile in the world. You will no longer understand the world's thinking for you are moving from death to life.

It can be very uncomfortable to get out of balance once you have experienced that peace that the world cannot give. We have to remain eternally unshaken, 'taking every thought captive to obey Christ'.

(2 Corinthians 10.5)

He Who Loves Us

The meaning of our time of trial here below is not to give us the chance to earn a reward but to teach us how to love, to enable us to enter into a true loving relationship with God, in which our response to him is a truly personal free response. If God keeps us in the dark this is not because he wishes to keep his distance from us, it is in order to lead us to a deeper communion with himself through humility.

We must trust in the Lord. Let him act. He can use the darkness to lead us further into the mystery of his presence. All that his presence is for us can be expressed in a simple attitude of waiting. We cry to someone, who is not far off, but is himself present in our cry. He is there and he holds us. His presence is more powerful than the darkness. Praying is to live in the sight of him who by his love makes us what we are. We must be obedient to him. We cry to the Lord who lives in the depths of our heart and who is one with our deepest being. We have only to listen to him. It is like listening to silence. A silent cry, simple, peaceful, an act of faith ... Everything subsists in him and through him. He surrounds us.

GEORGES LeFEBVRE

Send thy Holy Spirit, and they shall be created; and renew
the face of the earth.

Turn again, O Lord, how long? And be entreated for thy
servant.

The crooked places shall be made straight, and the rough
places plain.

O Lord my God, save thy servant, who putteth her* trust
in thee.

Be unto her*, O Lord, a pillar of strength against the face
of the enemy.

Let the enemy in nowise prevail against her*, and let not
the son of iniquity go about to offend her*.

*or his/him

FROM THE OFFICE FOR THE RECEPTION OF CONVERTS

Eastern Orthodox Church

I must have sung this hymn all through Presbyterian childhood, yet it is only now that I realize the beauty of the words. I use them as a prayer for calm and to bring us back into God's peace.

Dear Lord and Father of mankind,
Forgive our foolish ways.
Re-clothe us in our rightful mind;
In purer lives our service find,
In deeper reverence, praise.

In simple trust like theirs who heard,
Behind the Syrian sea.
The gracious calling of the Lord,
Let us, like them, without a word
Rise up and follow Thee.

Drop Thy still dews of quietness
Till all our strivings cease;
Take from our souls the strain and stress
And let our ordered lives confess
The beauty of Thy peace.

Breathe through the heats of our desire
Thy coolness and Thy balm,
Let sense be dumb, let flesh retire;
Speak through the earthquake wind and fire,
O Still small voice of calm!

(JOHN WHITTIER 1807–82)

... Life is given to us to learn to believe. Everything that happens, however upsetting, should lead us further in our faith.

GEORGES LEFEBVRE

There is only one way to overcome suffering, and that is to unite with God ... God himself steps in and helps us to carry it, even, in effect, carries it for us ... God becomes like a garment clothing us, so that anything which touches us touches him first. Therefore, when it reaches us, its character has changed, through the fact that it has passed through God, and has become impregnated, so to speak, with his flavour.

CYPRIAN SMITH

God in the Desert

The Apple of my Eye

When in the wilderness my people faced
The agony of desert place and howling waste.
There I encircled you with love divine
And gently sought you, dearest child of mine.
I know the desert places you have known.
I came to seek you, loved you, as my own.
There I encircled you in wilderness
And sought to touch you with my love's caress.
There in that desert place so harsh and dry
I kept you even as 'the apple of my eye'.
There like an eagle fluttering o'er its young
I flew beneath you while you fearful clung,
Spreading my pinions 'neath you, angel's wings.
I bore you up majestic, King of Kings.
I made you ride on high in realms of grace
Until at last you saw my Father's Face.
I fed you sweetest honey from the rock,
Curds from the herd and milk from my dear flock.

Yes, I the Shepherd God, the Great I AM
Have journeyed with you through your desert, precious
    lamb
There on dark Calvary I shed my blood
And gave my life for you, The Lamb of God
For bread of life I gave you finest wheat
And for your thirst the gift of wine so sweet
Red blood of grape, you drank, crushed on the precious
    vine
O taste and see, this is my Love Divine.
I in the wilderness and the desert place,
Have come to you, my wounded child, with grace,
Grace now sufficient I your Lord am nigh
I smile on you in love, the 'apple of my eye'.

DAVID PAYNE

(based on Deuteronomy 32:9–14)

Let nothing disturb thee
Nothing affright thee;
All things are passing;
God never changeth;
Patient endurance
Attaineth to all things;
Who God possesseth
In nothing is wanting
Alone God sufficeth.

(suggested to me by Lord Runcie)

Make thy face to shine upon thy servant;
and teach me thy statutes.

(Psalm 119.135)

In our natural selves, we do not have unlimited capacity to forgive, but God's love is infinite. If there is anything we cannot forgive, then we should begin by asking God to forgive on our behalf. It takes real strength to forgive: if we cannot, then we need to call on God's strength. This requires humility, for we are in effect admitting our weakness. The most important step is to give the problem to him. It is quite wonderful how this simple act of faith brings light into the situation ...

Forgiveness is an expression of love. It has the ability to heal and to bring hope: when people whose relatives have been murdered talk openly of forgiveness, it brings an extraordinary lightness into the situation. So much conflict is based on an inability to forgive: on a pathological need to remember past crimes, which can only lead to new griefs. There is no forgiveness without forgetting: it is a process of letting go completely. If we follow Christ's example, then we, too, can bring light and hope to resolve apparently intractable difficulties.

ROBERT BARNES

Continue in the struggle of your work. Descend into the sea of life and your endeavours. You will see Him Who is Risen on the shore. And coming out of the boat with a draught of fish in the nets of quest, you will find on the shore food ready to eat – 'a piece of broiled fish and of an honeycombe' – which will sweeten your mouth's bitterness and support your heart.

And no one will ask Him Who He is; since you will be certain that it is the Risen Lord, Who blesses and sanctifies the universe.

Then, discovering the hidden secrets of His love and compassion, you will proceed in the light of His face, and you will know Him as perfect God and perfect man, as the Alpha and Omega of history and of your life.

You will remember that at one time you thought that He had abandoned you as you hung on a cross of woes. However, it was precisely then that He was the more watchful beside you, fashioning the mystery of your salvation.

Now, as we have experienced the Resurrection, be certain that the Lord Who died and rose from the dead was, is and will remain with us all days, until the end of the centuries, as the unique hope and the salvation of us and of all mankind to the furthest parts of the earth.

Christ is risen from the dead and life rules!

To Him be the glory and the power to the ages. Amen.

VARTHOLOMAEOS

Archbishop of Constantinople
and Oecumenical Patriarch

Love

And now these three remain, faith, hope and love.
But the greatest of these is love.

(1 Corinthians 13)

Love in the West has been separated from the spiritual and therefore debased. We see around us the tasteless, decadent, distortions of love. A love that has lost its meaning.

Two thousand years ago something wonderful happened. God became Man. Jesus Christ became operative, enclosed in the physical body. Body and spirit act upon one another restoring wholeness and perfecting love. Man fell from grace but Christ's birth restored that grace. Love heals differences, unites nations and transfigures. It is like dew descending upon the earth.

Pure love is a state of oneness when all conflicting elements are stilled.

We are put upon this earth a little space to learn to bear the beams of love.

WILLIAM BLAKE

(suggested to me by the Right Revd. Richard Chartres, Bishop of London)

For each of us – perhaps once or twice only in the whole course of our life – there have been sudden moments of discovery when we have seen disclosed the deepest being and truth of another, and we have experienced his or her inner life as if it were our own, and this encounter with the true personhood of another is, once more, a contact with the transcendent and timeless, with something stronger than death. To say to another, with all our heart, 'I love you', is to say, 'You will never die'.

BISHOP KALLISTOS OF DIOKLEIA

The Orthodox Way

In the person I love is the One I am seeking. If I find myself loving a person it is only because I am trying to find, in and beyond that person, the God who is Love.

Every experience of love gives us yet another glimpse of the meaning of love in God himself.

Human love is the instrument we can use to explore the mystery of love which God is.

Human love reflects divine love and, indeed, transmits it.

BASIL HUME
The Mystery of Love

If I speak in the tongues of men and of angels, but have not love, I am a noisy gong or a clanging cymbal. And if I have prophetic powers, and understand all mysteries and all knowledge, and if I have all faith, so as to remove mountains, but have not love, I am nothing. If I give away all I have, and if I deliver my body to be burned, but have not love, I gain nothing.

Love is patient and kind; love is not jealous or boastful; it is not arrogant or rude. Love does not insist on its own way; it is not irritable or resentful, it does not rejoice at wrong, but rejoices in the right. Love bears all things, believes all things, hopes all things, endures all things.

Love never ends; as for prophecies, they will pass away. For our knowledge is imperfect and our prophecy is imperfect; but when the perfect comes the imperfect will pass away. When I was a child I spoke like a child, I thought like a child, I reasoned like a child; when I became a man I gave up childish ways. For now we see in a mirror dimly, but then face to face. Now I know in part; then I shall understand fully, even as I have been fully understood. So faith, hope, love abide, these three; but the greatest of these is love.

(I CORINTHIANS 13)

If the lover recognizes that the love with which and in which he beholds the beloved is a divine quality, he will then be seeing the beloved in God. He will be seeing her in the light of the love that in its essence is divine. He will not be loving her therefore outside or apart from God. In the fallen state – or with the profane type of consciousness – it is quite possible for a man and a woman to love each other outside and apart from God, at least where their own awareness and intentions are concerned, and to see each other as beings that have no relationship with God and are quite independent of Him. But in the paradisal state, man and woman love each other in God, aware that it is only by being in God that they can love at all.

Nor is it simply in God that they love each other. For possessing as they do a spiritual form of consciousness they know that everything that exists is a self-articulation or self-revelation of the Divine. Everything is an unveiling of God, a theophany in which God discloses Himself in His own image. Hence in loving each other what they love is God as He has revealed Himself in each of them to the other.

PHILIP SHERRARD

The Sacred in Life and Art

In his great love God was unwilling to restrict our freedom, even though he had the power to do so. He has left us to come to him by the love of our heart alone.

ISAAC OF NINEVEH

Ascetic Treatises

In God, the 'eros desire' is outgoing, ecstatic. Because of it lovers no longer belong to themselves but to those whom they love. God also goes out of himself ... when he captivates all creatures by the spell of his love and his desire ... In a word, we might say that Beauty-and-Goodness is the object of the eros desire and is the eros desire itself ...

DIONYSIUS THE AREOPAGITE

Divine Names

If you want to preserve love as God has asked, do not let your brother go to bed at night with a feeling of bitterness towards you. Do not, for your part, retire to rest with a feeling of bitterness towards him but go and be reconciled with your brother and then you will come to offer to Christ, with a pure conscience and in fervent prayer, the gift of love.

MAXIMUS THE CONFESSOR

Eros and Agape in Divine and Human Love

Eros is transformed by Agape, the spiritual love that comes from above:

The Fathers do not oppose these terms. *Agape* without *eros* would remain weak, powerless, mere moonshine, just as *eros* without *agape* would be a dark destructive force ... Together eros and agape constitute a creative virility, like the sun, joining heaven to earth.

OLIVIER CLÉMENT

The Roots of Christian Mysticism

Love for God is ecstatic, making us go out from ourselves; it does not allow the lover to belong any more to himself, but he belongs only to the Beloved.

DIONYSIUS THE AREOPAGITE

Thirst after Jesus and he will satisfy you with his love.

ST ISAAC THE SYRIAN

The truth that knowledge, in the deepest sense, means communion is constantly affirmed in the Bible. When the Book of Genesis, for example, tells us that Adam 'knew' Eve his wife, it is not talk about scientific, philosophical, or theological knowledge. It is talking about knowledge through communion, in this case communion of the flesh, consummated by a man and a woman within a marital relationship. But the same word, 'knowledge', is often used to refer to communion with God as well. When the prophets talk of 'knowing' the Lord, this, again, has nothing to do with science, philosophy, or theology.

Jacob and Job come to know the Lord, to unite with him and resemble him, by wrestling with him intently in the darkness. Knower and known often have to experience the clash of their difference and separateness, in order to find their ground of union and likeness.

Knowledge of God, then, means union with God, a kind of union which leads us to actually resemble God in some measure, to become to a certain extent like him. It is something which the Scriptures themselves call upon us to attempt. 'You, therefore, must be perfect,' says Jesus, 'as your heavenly Father is perfect.'

CYPRIAN SMITH
The Way of Paradox

If the face of someone we love ... makes us happy, how great will be the power of the Lord when he comes secretly to dwell in the soul that is pure?

Love is an abyss of light, a fountain of fire. The more it flows the more burning the thirst for it becomes ... that is why love is an everlasting progression.

JOHN CLIMACUS

I attain God in those who I love to the same degree in which, we, myself and they, become more and more spiritual. In the same way I grasp Him in the Beautiful and Good in proportion as I pursue these further and further with progressively purified faculties.

PIERRE TEILHARD DE CHARDIN

Le Milieu Divin

We only love if we have first been loved. Hear what the apostle John has to say. He it was who leant on the Master's heart and resting there drank in heavenly secrets ... Among the other secrets which the great seer drew from that source he showed us this: 'We love him because he first loved us' (1 John 4–10). Ask how anyone can love God and you will find no other answer than this: God first loved us. He whom we love has given himself first. He has given himself so that we may love him. What was his gift? The apostle Paul states it more clearly: 'God's love has been poured into our hearts'. By what means? Through us perhaps? No. Through whom then? 'Through the Holy Spirit, which has been given to us.' (Romans 5.5) ... You do not see God. Love and you possess him ... for God offers himself to us at once.

AUGUSTINE OF HIPPO

St Gregory of Nyssa has commented upon the Song of Songs, in which he sees the mystical marriage of the soul (and the Church) with God. The lover who pursues the beloved is the soul seeking its God. The beloved rises and escapes, God does the same; the more the soul knows Him, the more He escapes, and the more it loves Him. The more God satisfies it with His presence, the more it thirsts for a presence which is more total, and rushes headlong in pursuit. The more it is filled with God, the more it discovers Him transcendent. Thus the soul is penetrated with the divine presence but sinks ever deeper into the inexhaustible essence, inaccessible in as much as it is essence. Thus this pursuit becomes unending, and in this infinite dilation of the soul where love unceasingly overflows and renews itself from 'beginning to beginning,' Gregory sees the Christian notion of beatitude. If one knew the very nature of God, one would be God.

VLADIMIR LOSSKY

Orthodox Theology

Some people say that The Fathers of the Church are 'dry' and 'difficult to approach'. In the book *From Glory to Glory* St Gregory of Nyssa has a wonderful reaction to the Song of Solomon. He writes in beautiful language, spilling over with enthusiasm and allegory and virility and joy. So different from the legalistic, measured and pragmatic approach that we sometimes encounter in Western Christianity. He isn't tied *to* the Scriptures he is saturated *in* the Scriptures, with all the creative freedom of God's glory. Like the buds of springtime which cannot be contained.

The voice of my beloved!
Behold, he comes,
leaping upon the mountains,
bounding over the hills.
My beloved is like a gazelle,
or a young stag.
Behold, there he stands behind our wall,
gazing in at the windows,
looking through the lattice.
My beloved speaks and says to me;
Arise, my love, my fair one,
and come away;
for lo, the winter is past,
the rain is over and gone.
The flowers appear on the earth,
the time of singing has come,
and the voice of the turtledove
is heard in our land.
The fig tree puts forth its figs,
and the vines are in blossom;
they give forth fragrance.
Arise, my love, my fair one,
and come away.

Song of Songs 2:1–13

O my dove, in the clefts of the rock,
in the covert of the cliff,
let me see your face,
let me hear your voice
for your voice is sweet,
and your face is comely.
Catch us the foxes,
the little foxes,
that spoil the vineyard
for our vineyards are in blossom.
My beloved is mine and I am his,
he pastures his flock among the
lilies.
Until the day breathes
and the shadows flee,
turn, my beloved, be like a gazelle,
or a young stag upon rugged
mountains.

SONG OF SONGS: 2:14—17

And so He says: Arise and come. What power there is in this command! For indeed the voice of the Lord is a voice of power as the Psalmist has said: Behold he will give to his voice the voice of power (Psalm 67.34) and again: He spoke and they were made: he commanded and they were created (Psalm 32.9). So too He speaks to His reclining bride: Arise: and again Come – and straightway does His word become deed. For no sooner does she receive the power of the Word than she rises, approaches and draws near to the Light.

Now, how can you see a beautiful image in a mirror unless it has received the impression of a beautiful form? So it is with the mirror of human nature: it cannot become beautiful until it draws near to the Beautiful and becomes transformed by the image of the divine Beauty.

GREGORY OF NYSSA

Glory to Glory

The Winter is Now Past

The Word has spoken to the bride, calling her my love because she is close to Him, and 'my dove' because she is beautiful. He now goes on to say that the sadness of winter no longer dominates our souls. For the cold cannot resist the rays of the sun.

In wintertime everything that is lovely withers away. All the leaves, which are the natural crown of the beauty of the trees, fall from the branches and are mingled with earth. The song of the birds is silent, the nightingale flies away, the swallow sleeps and the dove leaves its nest ...

GREGORY OF NYSSA

Glory to Glory

From Dove to Dove

... The soul grows by its constant participation in that which transcends it ...

We see the Word, then, leading the bride up a rising staircase, as it were, up to the heights by the ascent of perfection. The Word first sends forth a ray of light 'through the windows' of the Prophets and 'through the lattices' of the Law and the commandments. Then He bids the bride draw near to the Light and then to become beautiful by being changed, in the light, into the form of the Dove.

GREGORY OF NYSSA

The Little Foxes

And so the pure Bridegroom accepts the just request of His Bride: but before revealing Himself openly. He first urges the hunters to catch the foxes to prevent them from spoiling the growth of His vine to maturity, and He says: 'Catch us the little foxes that destroy the vines.' ...

He does not say: Hunt the boar of the forest that ravages God's vine, nor the solitary wildboar, nor the roaring lion, nor the great whale, nor the sea serpent ...

(Bearing in mind that St Gregory of Nyssa lived between 330 and 395 AD I have heard a more contemporary interpretation of 'the little foxes' from Dr Edward Short. He looks upon them as the remaining faults in us that have to be removed before perfection is reached. Our words perhaps. Kindly, loving words encourage growth and a feeling of well being – unkind words are debilitating and destructive. The first give life, the second take it away. He would add that our human effort is insufficient to do this but the Lord can do it as we let Him come into our hearts.)

'No-one has ever seen God, but if we love one another, God lives in us and his love is made complete in us.' So, 'Let us love one another, for love comes from God. Everyone who loves has been born of God and knows God. Whoever does not love does not know God, because God is love. This is how God showed his love among us: He sent his one and only Son into the world that we might live through him.' (1 John 4)

As well as the story of love between Solomon and his bride, the Song of Songs speaks of Jesus' love for us: 'You have stolen my heart with one glance of your eyes.' (4.9) If this is how he feels when we look at him fleetingly, how must he feel when we gaze deep into his face and tell him that we love him! ... 'Arise, my darling, my beautiful one, and come with me. See! The winter is past; the rains are over and gone. Flowers appear on the earth; the season of singing has come, and the cooing of doves is heard again in our land.' (2.10–12)

'And now these three remain: faith, hope and love. But the greatest of these is love.' (1 Corinthians 13)

ROBERT BARNES

The Wise Men travelled a long way and nobody knows the difficulties they had to overcome. Each of us also travels as they did. They were loaded with gifts, gold for the King, frankincense for the God, myrrh for the man who was to suffer death. Where can we get gold, frankincense and myrrh, we who are indebted for everything to God? We know that everything we possess has been given us by God and is not even ours for ever or with certainty. Everything can be taken away from us except love, and this is what makes love unique and something we can give. Everything else, our limbs, our intelligence, our possessions can be taken by force from us, but with regard to love, there is no means of getting it, unless we give it. In that sense we are free with regard to loving, in a way in which we are not free in other activities of soul or body. Although fundamentally even love is a gift of God, because we cannot produce it out of ourselves, yet, once we possess it, it is the only thing that we can withhold or offer.

METROPOLITAN ANTHONY OF SOUROZH

Living Prayer

The first rays of pure youthful love can transfigure, in the eyes of those who love, the whole surrounding scenery, the simplest event of life, the whole texture of life, with a glamour of beauty, with the shine of the beloved Presence.

NICHOLAS ARSENIEV
Revelation of Life Eternal

God is absolute beauty because he is absolute personal existence. As such, he awakens our desire, sets it free and draws it to himself. He sets beings within their limits but he calls them into communion with one another without confusing them. Being himself beyond movement or rest, he gives to each creature an identity that is exact and distinct, but is nevertheless capable of development when brought to life by the dynamic power of love.

OLIVIER CLÉMENT
The Roots of Christian Mysticism

Death and the Immortality of the Human Soul

Death is not an end but a stage in the destiny of man.

METROPOLITAN ANTHONY OF SOUROZH

In the course of one's life one sows seeds. These seeds develop in the souls of other men and affect their destiny, and the fruit that is born of these seeds truly belongs not only to those who bear it but also to those who sow.

METROPOLITAN ANTHONY OF SOUROZH

Living Prayer

... I remember observing the garden poppy. When it flowers it is scarlet and flamboyant. Then the crumpled petals wither and fall away. There is a certain ugliness in the first death. It looks like the end, yet a few days later everything has changed. In the place where the petals have been there is a star-shaped lid, perfect in its mathematical precision and timing, holding the seeds of a new beginning. From this I grasped that life 'continually assumes new forms' far in advance of our human intellect.

The Greek Butterfly

My younger daughter, Charlotte had pulled off the M4 on to the hard shoulder because her car had overheated. She was with a girlfriend waiting for the AA tanned and happy from a holiday in Spain, shiny plastic bags filled with shells and presents. She had just rung to say they were on their way home. They never made it. A lorry ploughed into them from behind, tearing off the roof of the car like a sardine tin. One girl, miraculously, survived, but for Charlotte it was instant oblivion. An unnatural, impersonal and very contemporary death, grotesque in its violence.

We sat by her still body in the Intensive Care Unit of the Princess Margaret Hospital in Swindon. She was wired into technology, flawless in her beauty, in spite of the deadly head and chest wounds. The smell of petrol permeated the area around her bed. We held hands, we prayed, we sent beams of love, and each member of the family lived through a lonely agony, made bearable because it was unbearable in its magnitude.

A week later she was buried in the graveyard beside the old Manor where we used to live. Steeple Ashton is a small village in Wiltshire. The church, like a cathedral, was packed with people. Sarah and I filled it with flowers — white blossoms. Like a wedding. As an actress, Charlotte had just been making a name for herself. In a series called 'Tripods' she played the daughter of a Count and Countess. In a hauntingly beautiful death scene, she was raised into the sky for a new life in the City of Gold. It was shown on television the day after her funeral. There were too many coincidences ...

If someone dies who is young and good and vital and beautiful and if you love her, there is no way you can accept that death is the end or that her loss is something other than very sacred. We are being hurled into an advanced stage of spiritual growth.

It has been said that 'part of a pattern is nothing in itself. It is only when we see the whole of it that we understand the reason.' We have to grasp the event with an eternal level of perception. We cannot afford to stay for too long in the grimmest of material circumstance; to ponder too much, to brood, to sustain anger, destroys us. To be alert and observant is an essential part of the experience.

In the West our eternal values are often dormant. We have to do something very difficult. We must move right away from material thinking and human logic, to a much deeper understanding of the whole significance of Christ's death and resurrection.

In dealing with Charlotte's death, and there are many similar deaths in the world in which we live, the darkness had to be dissolved and the horror of it transfigured. I will keep to one incident. On at least three occasions Charlotte had said she would die young. There was nothing morbid in her announcement; it was simply a statement. I told her not to be frightened of death, but to think of it as 'change' – like a caterpillar changing into a butterfly. The analogy of the butterfly was to have unforeseen implications. Charlotte had never been to Greece, in fact she had hardly ever been abroad, and yet her drawings at this time showed strangely classical, paradisical landscapes. After her death we found a notebook. It was the sort of notebook any teenager might keep; titles of books, dance routines, French verbs – and yet there were words of extraordinary beauty and depth as though she had already touched a holy place, like a foretaste of the Kingdom. As though the change that St Paul describes in 1 Corinthians 15 had already begun. As though God was preparing her.

My elder daughter Sarah and I followed the drawings and went to Greece with our mutual friend, John Tavener. His mother had died about the same time so we were all in the same boat, so to speak. One day a beautiful butterfly lay dead at Sarah's feet in an Aegina garden. It was the largest butterfly we had ever seen and striped like a dress that Charlotte had worn. Sarah lifted it up gently because it seemed to symbolize Charlotte's death. We took the dead butterfly to the little white Monastery dedicated to St Nectarios, the newest Saint in Greece. We lit candles and Sarah laid the butterfly among the flowers on his Holy Table. We prayed and cried and felt a peace from that little Church that was beyond all understanding.

Later as we lay on the beach with our feet in the water and our heads among the sandflies I said it was strange that a butterfly, like a soul, was attracted to beautiful things – jasmine, hibiscus, oleander. It would never come to a beach to land on seaweed. But it did – an exact replica of the enormous butterfly we had left with St Nectarios hovered on the seaweed in front of us. Then it just flew away over the sea.

Our visit to the tomb of St Nectarios had a profound effect on me. I knelt beside the cold marble where jasmine, white roses and camelias lay in profusion, sweet smelling and familiar ... There was a feeling of weightlessness, of timelessness, and of infinite grace. We lit a candle in the small courtyard, leaving a flame in the bright sunlight. White walls, black dresses, scarlet geraniums – the colours of death and perpetual life.

I am more cautious now with anything that can be termed a vision but in the early evening as I lay resting in the white cell of my room, with the bougainvillea trailing over the arched window, I shut my eyes. And then I saw face after face of extraordinary beauty and purity, one dissolving into the next. They were Apostolic, Saint-like, Christ-like faces . . .

At night, to the sound of cicadas, we would eat against the flat biblical backcloth of the sea. The sun, as it went down looked spherical instead of flat, as though another dimension was creeping into our lives. We could have been beside the Sea of Genneseret. The fishermen and the fishes were there, and the symbolic bread and wine, always shared.

People here talked about God without inhibition. Macarios the Great, Gregory Palamas, Symeon the New Theologian, Basil the Great had never come into our conversation before.

Gradually the darkness was scattered. In the same way as we see an icon with its perspective widening into eternity, rather than narrowing into worldly distance, so we were led from time that is finite into an understanding of time that is eternal.

Both Sarah and I converted to Orthodoxy. We had discovered the writings of the Holy Fathers and felt drawn to a tradition where the wisdom and mystery were undiluted. In 1986 we were received into the Russian Orthodox Cathedral in London.

The seeds that Charlotte sowed in her short life bore such fruit that everything now is relative. The tragedy cannot be taken away, but the quality of suffering changed completely, and the presence of God was unmistakable.

To a Greek Butterfly

From oleander to hibiscus
Like a soul removed from earth
You leave squalor and decay
Choosing only perfection
With the briefest camouflage of colour
You bring the essence of Angels to this unseeing world.

MARGARET LONG

(written in Aegina)

Charlotte

Charlotte's words written a few weeks before her death:

I awake in a spectrum of light and colour. I try to pass through it but it makes me acknowledge it. I go back and start again and new colours are inside me.

I saw an egg one spring evening, vivid blue, like sky in the lake, with dark speckles for my trees. I fought to change the route, but all I could do was watch the path diminish through the trees like a vibration of music dissolving and diffusing in the air.

Levels of inadequate comprehension, they drift through me like the quality of light and I feel happy . . .

I walk through levels of unimaginable description. I catch the moon in my mind like an engulfment of new life and I lie down to die, to prepare to live again.

I know something is happening that God has arranged.

Blessed is our God Always, now, and ever, and unto ages of ages. Amen.

... Blessed are those whom thou hast chosen and taken, O Lord. The remembrance of them is from generation to generation. Their souls shall dwell with the blessed. Alleluia. Alleluia. Alleluia.
O Thou who, with wisdom profound, mercifully orderest all things, who givest that which is expedient unto all men, thou Only Creator: Give rest, O Lord, to the souls of thy servants who have fallen asleep; For they have set their hope on thee, our Maker, the Author of our being, and our God. Glory to the Father, and to the Son, and to the Holy Spirit, now, and ever, and unto ages and ages.
Amen.

... Blessed art thou, O Lord; teach me thy statutes. The Choir of the Saints have found the Fountain of Life and the Door of Paradise. May I also find the right way, through repentance. I am a lost sheep. Call me, O Saviour, and save me.

Blessed art Thou, O Lord: teach me thy statutes. Give rest O God to the souls of Thy servants and set them in Paradise where the Choirs of the Saints and the Just shine like the stars. Give rest, O Lord, to Thy servants who have fallen asleep, and overlook all their offences. Glory be to the Father, and to the Son, and to the Holy Spirit, now, and ever, and unto ages of ages. Amen.

From the beautiful and moving Sung
Panikhida or Requiem Service, Eastern Orthodox Church

He who asserts that there is nothing after this life must assert that there is no God either ... For if there is nothing beyond death, then neither is there a God. For if God exists, He is just ... And if He is just, He gives to each what he deserves.

ST JOHN CHRYSOSTOM

Thank you Lord Jesus
for all you have given me,
for all you have taken away from me
and for all you have left me.

PRAYER OF ST THOMAS MORE

(*suggested to me by Father Augustine Hoey*)

Many prayers, at least in the West, are only for Christian dead – and of course so many people today want to pray for loved ones whose faith they have reason to doubt.

As with much of the ancient language in Orthodoxy it is sometimes archaic and unfamiliar, but that is, strangely enough, its beauty and strength. Nothing changes except perhaps, the way in which we die:

From *Canticle 1*

In the depth of Thy judgements, O Christ, with fullness of wisdom Thou hast preordained the end of each man's life, its appointed moment and its manner. Therefore, All-Merciful, at the judgement save those in every land whom the grave has hidden.

Give rest, O Lord, to the souls of Thy departed servants.

To those hidden by the deep or cut down in battle, swallowed by earthquake, murdered, or consumed by fire, grant in Thy mercy a place with the faithful and the righteous.

Give rest, O Lord, to the souls of Thy departed servants.

Overlooking all the transgressions of the flesh, our Saviour, in every age, by every nation of mankind, grant that, as they make their defence to Thee the Creator, they may stand before Thy judgement-seat uncondemned.

Glory be to the Father, and to the Son and to the Holy Spirit

Both now and ever and unto the Ages of Ages. Amen.

FROM THE LITURGY FOR 'SATURDAY OF THE DEAD'

(*suggested to me by The Revd. Father Anthony Grant, CR*)

From *Canticle 3*

To those who have been suddenly snatched away. Burnt up by lightening, frozen by the cold, or struck down by any other calamity, give rest, O God, when Thou shalt make trial of all things in the fire.

Those whom the creatures of the sea or the birds of the air have devoured, O Christ our God, raise up in glory on the Last Day, as Thou judgest right.

Glory be to the Father, and to the Son and to the Holy Spirit

Both now and ever and unto the Ages of Ages. Amen.

FROM THE LITURGY FOR 'SATURDAY OF THE DEAD'

(*suggested to me by The Revd. Father Anthony Grant, CR*)

From *Canticle 4*

Those who died in faith on the mountainside or the road, in the tombs or the desert, monks and married people, young and old, grant to them all, O Christ, a dwelling with Thy saints.

To those destroyed by the cold, killed by falling from their horse, overwhelmed by hail, snow or thunderstorms, crushed by stone or suffocated in the earth, give rest, O Christ our Saviour.

Glory be to the Father, and to the Son and to the Holy Spirit

Both now and ever and unto the Ages of Ages. Amen.

FROM THE LITURGY FOR 'SATURDAY OF THE DEAD'

(suggested to me by The Revd. Father Anthony Grant, CR)

The Judgement

Then the King will say to those at his right hand, 'Come, O blessed of my Father, inherit the Kingdom prepared for you from the foundation of the world; for I was hungry and you gave me food. I was thirsty and you gave me drink. I was a stranger and you welcomed me, I was naked and you clothed me, I was in prison and you came to me.' Then the righteous will answer Him. 'Lord, when did we see thee hungry and feed thee, or thirsty and give thee drink? And when did we see thee a stranger and welcome thee, or naked and clothe thee? And when did we see thee sick or in prison and visit thee?' And the King will answer them, 'Truly, I say to you, as you did it to one of the least of these my brethern, you did it to me.'

(MATTHEW 25:14–40)

At the time of Charlotte's death, and shortly after our visit to the Monastery of St Nectarios, John Tavener led Sarah and me to a bookshop, hidden away in Athens. We would never have found it on our own and we had to climb a staircase to get into it. It was there that I discovered a book by Constantine Cavarnos on seven philosophers of modern Greece discussing the nature and immortality of the human soul. This book was published for the first time in English and included statements from Western thinkers such as Emmerson. I was also to discover that St Nectarios, to whom we had been led in such a miraculous way, had written more on the immortality of the soul than any other Greek, living or dead.

On the Human Soul

The existence of the living soul is a solved problem for believers, but a hidden mystery for unbelievers.

God revealed to man his noble origin and made known to him the immortality of his soul, in order to attract him towards Himself ... and to lead him towards self-perfection.

A spirit that seeks the immortal cannot be mortal. Immortality presses towards immortality. The impetus of the spirit testifies to the immortal nature.

The all-good God would not have implanted in the heart of man an unfulfilled aspiration that renders him unhappy, unless He had reserved its fulfillment. Since it remains unfilfilled in this world, it follows that it will be fulfilled after man's departure from it.

ST NECTARIOS OF AEGINA

In the same vein as St Nectarios, Emmerson remarks:

There is nothing in nature capricious, or whimsical, or accidental, or unsupported. Nature never moves by jumps, but always in steady and supported advances. The implanting of a desire indicates that the gratification of the desire is in the constitution of the creature that feels it; the wish for food, the wish for motion, the wish for sleep, for society, for knowledge, are not random whims, but grounded in the structure of the creature, and meant to be satisfied by food, by motion, by sleep, by society, by knowledge. If there is the desire to live, and in larger sphere, with more knowledge and power, it is because life and knowledge and power, are good for us, and we are the natural depositories of these gifts. All I have seen teaches me to trust the Creator for all I have not seen. Whatever it be which the great Providence prepares for us, it must be something large and generous, and in the great style of his works. The future must be up to the style of our faculties − of memory, of hope, of imagination, of reason.

Reason is an instrument that helps the soul become conscious of its immortality while still in time ... Faith, however, is a leap beyond mere knowledge, is a self-affirmation of the value called *man* that relates man to eternity.

IOANNIS N. THEODORAKOPOULOS

'Those who do not believe in the immateriality and imperishability of the soul have not been present at the death of a genius; but I have been' wrote Arsene Houssaie. 'How many times didn't I hear Hugo [Victor Hugo] proclaiming and teaching the immortality of the soul. One evening he seemed to be asleep; but suddenly he raised his head and opened his still sparkling eyes. 'I am not asleep,' he said, 'but hear what is being said around me and most of all what is being said above us. Everything is luminous in my head; the earth still provides me with its saps, but a heavenly light of other worlds shines in my spirit. Perhaps you believe that the soul is a product of organic and bodily movements and functions. But then why is the mind brighter at this moment, when the powers of the body are vanishing? A heavy winter has come upon my bodily organism, but an eternal spring is preserved in my soul. The more I approach the end, the more clearly I discern the heavenly harmonies. For half a century I have been writing my ideas. I applied myself to history, philosophy, legends, traditions, songs, to every-thing knowable. Yet I have not expended even a thousandth part of the spiritual life within me. In the grave I will not say that I have ceased living, but that I have ended my day – for the new one begins the next day. The grave is not the end, but simply a transition.'

IOANNIS SKALTSOUNIS

No eye has seen,
no ear has heard,
no mind has conceived
what God has prepared for those who
love him.

(1 Corinthians 2.9)

Let not your heart be troubled; ye believe
in God, believe also in me.
In my Father's house are many mansions;
if it were not so, I would have told you.
I go to prepare a place for you.
And if I go and prepare a place for you,
I will come again, and receive you unto
myself; that where I am, there ye may be also.

(John 14:1–4)

Places of Prayer

Poustinia is the Russian word meaning desert. When you enter the *poustinia* you enter the orbit of God. You hold on to his coat. A thousand hands try to pull his coat out of your hands. You are free to give in to the temptation, to flee from the *poustinia* or to resist.

CATHERINE DE HUECK DOHERTY

So long as our view of Christian mysticism is based only on a study of the Catholic and Protestant mystics of the west, it will inevitably be lop-sided and incomplete. Even such glimpses into the hidden life of the Eastern Church as Cassian's Dialogues or the Greek Fathers give us, warn us that there another type of spiritual culture grew up; having its own particular riches, its own gifts to make to the total consciousness of the Church of Christ. But difficulties of language, and the formidably ceremonial exterior which is all that Orthodox Christianity shows to the uninitiated, have hitherto blocked the way to any deep understanding of its mystical experience: an experience which has developed without a break from that characterising Primitive Christianity, and sometimes contrasts with, sometimes completes and supports our own.

Orthodox Spirituality has, it seems to me, much to teach the modern West. The type of Christianity which most appeals to us tends more and more to be predominantly terrestrial and utilitarian in outlook ... (Orthodoxy, the Eucharist) points beyond the here and now to a transubstantiation of the whole material order; a veritable 'bringing in of the Kingdom of God.'

EVELYN UNDERHILL

from her Introduction to Nicholas Arseniev's
Mysticism and the Eastern Church

The Orthodox Christian reverently regards the Church as the House of God, as the embodiment of a different reality – that of the Heavenly future that mankind has yet to attain and towards which humanity is ever striving.

BISHOP SERAFIM OF ZURICH

In church God is at home, it is his place; he is not only the creator and the lord by right but he is recognized as such. Outside it he acts when he can and how he can; inside a church he has all power and all might and it is for us to come to him.

When we build a church or set apart a place of worship we do something which reaches far beyond the obvious significance of the fact. The whole world which God created has become a place where men have sinned; the devil has been at work, a fight is going on constantly; there is no place on this earth which has not been soiled by blood, suffering or sin. When we choose a minute part of it, calling upon the power of God himself, in rites which convey his grace to bless it, when we cleanse it from the presence of the evil spirit, and set it apart to be God's foothold on earth, we reconquer for God a small part of this desecrated world. We may say that this is a place where the kingdom of God reveals itself and manifests itself with power. When we come to church we should be aware that we are entering upon sacred ground, a place which belongs to God, and we should behave accordingly.

METROPOLITAN ANTHONY OF SOUROZH

Living Prayer

 117

A Church must be an oasis in the desert of today: (for the Orthodox) there must be icons and lamps burning before them, there must be a sanctuary where prayer is valid, there must be silence, mystery, and solitude in a world that has grown too noisy, too blatant and too over crowded.

There are many forms of oases in the deserts of today's world – rich Cathedrals, obscure Churches, monasteries, hermitages, cells, but what makes them pulsate with life and thus become places of spiritual refreshment is that there is a 'watcher and a holy one' (Daniel 4.13) keeping vigil, whose heart fails not in the darkest hour, who will 'not break the bruised reed, will not quench the smoking flax, who will not fail nor be discouraged'. (Isaiah 42.3) The world has need of such places and people; the desert will always cry out for an oasis, for the Lord who made it will one day re-make it according to Isaiah's prophecy: 'Behold I will do a new thing ... will even make a way in the wilderness and rivers in the desert.' (Isaiah 43.19)

Prayer must not be divorced from the Church but united with it, and the 'little sanctuaries' in our houses where we practise prayer must have the link with the Church which is the Body and Bride of Christ.

FATHER BARNABAS

a meditation on the word *Oasis*

Although we know that God is everywhere and fills all things, we know too the feeling, the recognition, we have in certain places where prayer has taken place. Places that have been uncontaminated by the world. An 'oasis', a place where holiness can be felt. I include a paragraph from an article I wrote in *The Times* referring to the Russian Orthodox Cathedral in Ennismore Gardens:

> Divine Liturgy in the Russian Orthodox Cathedral in Ennismore Gardens, London, is like walking into Constantinople. Nothing has changed since Byzantine times. The music, the words, the dignity, the simplicity, the scholarship and the timeless rhythm of eternity joins heaven to Earth. The candlelight and the calm presence of the icons introduce a reality and hierarchy of such holiness that faces, however plain in the worldly sense, are transfigured in prayer. It is a communion of saints where people stand as still as a forest, upheld by the deep joy and grace of Christ's presence.

We do not go to Church to have a moral uplift, though that does happen: we do not go to be edified though that happens also, but we do go to offer something to the Triune God in company with the Redeemed. So we are never alone in our worship; isolated Orthodox who pray are like the desert dwellers continually sustained in their solitude by unseen presences, and the very act of joining with them gives us the up-lift which we need to continue on life's pilgrimage.

... where there is no Church at hand each family should have its Icon Corner and there in great simplicity and sincerity offer up what prayers it can, the lamps lighted and the icons shedding a glory which transforms us.

We must always live in God's Presence – always be aware of His nearness – if we fail there must be instant repentance without delay. Then we must cultivate a sense of the presence of the Communion of Saints, especially the Holy Theotokos, the Angels – be aware of this army of bodiless Powers. Because it is a fact that as soon as we seriously begin the work of 'walking with God' we awake our enemies and a battleground is made in our own souls, inside us. This is where the Sacraments help and where we should have recourse to our spiritual guide, a soul-friend, who himself walks along this way, knows its dangers, and realizes that it is 'the narrow way that leads to life' (Matt.7.13–14) and because of his knowledge and love of us, is able to help us.

FATHER BARNABAS

Rationalists would reproach Orthodox believers for their excessive emphasis on ritual. Such a view, however, betrays a misconception of both ritual and its purpose. Just as a child's first awareness of nature predates any formal study of the world around us, ritual in the Church often introduces doctrine. Religion is not merely speculation on things divine; it must be a complete acceptance of Divinity, without reservation ... When a feeling of love overcomes us, we give it some outward expression, performing a sort of ritual as when a mother kisses and caresses her child. The same is true in religion. If we believe in an abstract God, ritual is inappropriate, but if our God is a living and personal Presence, then the need for ritual – for a visible manifestation of our love – becomes very real.

BISHOP SERAFIM OF ZURICH

The perspective in an icon is often back to front, widening into eternity rather than narrowing into worldly distance so that we are led into an eternal understanding of things. Icons are sometimes described as 'windows into Heaven', prayer reflecting God's Kingdom and bringing Heaven to earth.

An icon is a focus of real presence. St John Chrysostom advises us, before we start praying, to take our stand in front of an icon and to shut our eyes. He says 'shut your eyes', because it is not by examining the icon, by using it as a visual aid, that we are helped by it to pray. It is not a substantial presence in the sense in which the bread and wine are the body and blood of Christ. An icon is not, in this sense, Christ, but there is a mysterious link between the two. By the power of grace an icon participates in something which can best be defined in the words of Gregory Palamas as the energies of Christ, as the active power of Christ working for our salvation.

METROPOLITAN ANTHONY OF SOUROZH

An icon is painted as an act of worship. The wood is chosen and blessed, the paint is blessed, the man who wishes to paint prepares himself by fasting, by confession, by communion. He keeps ascetical rules while working and when his work is completed, it is blessed with holy water and *chrismated** (this last part of the blessing is now often omitted, unfortunately). Thus, by the power of the Holy Spirit, the icon becomes more than a painting. It is loaded with presence, imbued with the grace of the Spirit and linked with the particular saint it represents in and through the mystery of the communion of saints and the cosmic unity of all things. One cannot say of the icon that the indwelling of the saint is identical with or even similar to that which we find in the holy gifts, and yet it is a focus of real presence as it is experienced and taught by the (Orthodox) Church. An icon is not a likeness, it is a sign. Certain icons have been singled out by the power and wisdom of God to be miraculous icons. When you stand in their presence you feel challenged by them.

METROPOLITAN ANTHONY OF SOUROZH

Living Prayer

*blessed by a priest during Divine Liturgy .

 123

Russian Piety

... The liturgy of the Russian Orthodox Church is indeed a synthesis of art forms. Beauty, like the glory of God, suffuses the church. Architecture and frescoes, icons ... the choir ... the poetry of hymns, the richly designed and crafted vestments, the graceful movements of the celebrants, the glow of icon lamps and candles, and the sweet smell of incense – all blend together in homage to God and beauty.

This ensemble is not merely soothing and symbolic, it is also dynamic and effective ... in the words of Dostoyevsky: 'Beauty will save the world.' This sensuous beauty is a manifestation of spiritual beauty considered one of the criteria of Orthodox ecclesiasticism (*tserkounost*). 'What then is *tserkounost*,' asks Florensky, who in turn answers: 'It is new life, life of the spirit.' What then is the criterion of the authenticity of this new life? It is beauty.

Bishop Serafim of Zurich

When you enter the *poustinia* you enter the orbit of God. You hold on to his coat. A thousand hands try to pull his coat out of your hands. You are free to give in to the temptation, to flee from the *poustinia* or to resist.

The word *poustinia* is Russian meaning 'desert'. It is an ordinary word. If I were a little Russian girl, and a teacher during a geography lesson asked me to name a desert, I might say, *Saharskaya Poustinia* – the Sahara Desert. That's what it really means. It also has another connotation, as so many words have. It also means the desert of the Fathers of the Desert, who in ages past went away from every-thing and settled there. In the Western sense of the word, it would mean a place to which a hermit goes and, hence, it could be called a hermitage.

The word to the Russian means much more than a geographical place. It means a quiet, lonely place that people wish to enter, to find the God who dwells within them. It also means truly isolated, lonely places to which specially called people would go as hermits, and would seek God in solitude, silence and prayer for the rest of their lives.

However, a *poustinia* was not necessarily completely away from the haunts of men. Some people had reserved, in their homes, a small room to which they went to pray ... which some might call a *poustinia*.

CATHERINE DE HUECK DOHERTY

Poustinia

The Russians say, 'If you have a recollected and quiet spirit, people will gather around you when you speak.' Why is this? Because you won't be speaking; He will.

With this surrender of my words to His Word comes the gift of discernment, the gift of knowing what to say to each person. Because His Word has taken over my words, a clarity enters into me which enables me to see the heart of the other and to know what to say. When we are surrendered to His Word, the gift of discernment will make our words quite flexible. Now compassionate, now merciful, now most direct – the clarity which His Word has brought and which I have accepted at great pain to myself now goes out as a ray of light to somebody else ... this is one of the charisms of the *poustinia*, ... The *poustinik* must learn to speak anew, out of his heart, the words God gives him. It's like learning to talk all over again.

I know that in the *poustinia* lies the answer that the world is seeking today. The world knows ABOUT God. Because it only knows ABOUT Him, it can reject Him, ignore Him, be indifferent to Him, recrucify Him a thousand times a day in the neighbour. But if the world knew Him through his own revelation of Himself to us in the *poustinia* of our hearts, then it could not reject Him. Once known in this way, He would not be able to be rejected. Then love would enter the world through us. We could speak His word to the world if we lived in the *poustinia* of our hearts ...

CATHERINE DE HUECK DOHERTY

Poustinia

126

... a person is led into the *poustinia* to become empty. This emptiness results in the ability to listen. If the *poustinik* is attentive and listening in his *poustinia*, he will also know when he must speak outside the *poustinia*. They will not be so much his words as the words of Christ. The courage to speak these words is part of the *kenosis*, part of the emptiness. The words of man suddenly become the Word of God. God takes over, and all our tiny, peanut words suddenly coalesce and in some miraculous way become The Word.

The role of the *poustinik*, is allowing himself to quite literally 'shut up', to become silent. This means giving up YOUR words. Folding the wings of your intellect means giving up the birthplace, the origin, the source of your own words. What for? To become merely dumb, without any speech at all? No. It's in order that The Word might take over your words. This is the reason why you are silent in total solitude. It's a strange silence in which you lay your words out on that altar so that you don't have any more of your own words. The birthplace of your own words is now empty.

CATHERINE DE HUECK DOHERTY

Poustinia

Bitter Waters

When a man has given up the Egyptian pleasures to which he had been enslaved before crossing the water, his life seems at first bitter and disagreeable now his pleasures have been taken away. But once the wood is cast into the waters, that is, once he unites himself to the mystery of the resurrection, which had its beginning in the wood (and by the wood here you surely understand the Cross), then the life of virtue becomes sweeter and more refreshing than all the sweetness that makes the sense tingle with pleasure, because it has been seasoned by our hope in the things to come.

Gregory of Nyssa

On Mount Athos is a bleak, exposed hillside known as Karoulia which in a book was once, I believe, called The Holy Planet Purgatory. More often it is known as The Desert. This place on earth is named for a place in the human heart, and it might seem that it was so named because of its topography. It consists of steep rocky slopes at the storm-blasted tip of Mount Athos. Before the time of Alexander and Aristotle, it was at the foot of these cliffs that Xerxes' fleet was wrecked. He lost twenty thousand men.

Robin Amis

A Different Christianity

In Mount Athos's one primitive hotel, four iron beds, four rickety chairs, pillow, blanket, a small table, an oil lamp and several tacked-up postcards of icons made up the furnishings. 'Like monastery' said the owner optimistically. I lay down, drew the blanket over my head, and attempted to take my siesta. It was around three in the afternoon, and the day stretched interminably before me.

It was during this long day, with no monastic spirituality to compensate for the barren environment, that I met in full strength Saint Gregory's 'bitter waters' of separation from the outside world, and so learned something about how, in our Western world, we use our comforts and our distractions to hide from ourselves and our own emptiness. (These are what the monk leaves behind him when he is said to leave the 'world.') At the same time I learned to value more fully the unique riches of the monastic world that had been so kindly opened to me.

At times like this, no matter what the external circumstance, the pattern is always the same. I would first face the freewheeling thoughts of my own mind and then, when I managed to step back from these thoughts that continued to run through my head, I would meet this emptiness, this bitterness that emerges when one faces an immediate future that is not only without pleasures and without distractions, but also offers no certainty of something to replace those distractions.

ROBIN AMIS

A Different Christianity

129

On every visit to Athos, I have at some time rediscovered the 'well of bitter waters' that was first described by a Father of the Church so long ago. In the monasteries, I have also discovered the palliative for this unease. There, as Saint Gregory of Nyssa put it, they possess the wood of the cross, symbolic of the living liturgy, of the Resurrection itself, to sweeten the bitterness. Here, I am now convinced, is an elixir, a medicine for this bitterness. This was why the early Fathers could recommend exile, could recommend the solitary life. But we cannot easily retain this state in our ordinary lives, and so when I go there again it is only after withstanding this inner desert, this sense of emptiness, for a day, sometimes for several days, that I discover once again the inner well of peace and happiness that makes it possible for the monk to live his hard and outwardly unrewarding life. So much does the effect of our ordinary life cling to us – or to be more exact, so much do we cling to our ordinary life – that this benefit has often emerged only toward the end of my visits. This is why the Gospel According to Thomas says: 'The fox has his lair, the bird has his nest, but the Son of Man has no place to lay his head.'

ROBIN AMIS

A Different Christianity

The Desert Fathers believed that the wilderness had been created as supremely valuable in the eyes of God precisely because it has no value to men. The wasteland was the land that could never be wasted by men because it offered them nothing. There was nothing to attract them. There was nothing to exploit. The desert was the region in which the Chosen People had wandered for forty years, cared for by God alone. They could have reached the Promised Land in a few months if they had travelled directly to it. God's plan was that they should learn to love Him in the wilderness and that they should always look back upon the time in the desert as the idyllic time of their life with Him alone.

THOMAS MERTON

Thoughts in Solitude

The Fishermen's Café

In Greece I found an unexpected and unpredictable depth of imagery which seemed to reinforce faith. Everyday life spilled into the Churches and the Liturgy spilled into everyday life. I remember visiting a fishermen's cafe which was almost black inside. Dark as a cave. Tourists did not go there for they were dazzled by the glitter of the shops on either side, selling gold bangles, mugs, plaster moulds of Apollo and Aphrodite and green fluorescent milk shakes.

Inside the cafe I watched the dark, intelligent eyes of the fishermen and the absorbing intensity of the conversation and asked a friend what they were talking about. The answer was: 'What they are always talking about – Socrates, Plato and God.'

There was a biblical Last Supper atmosphere as they came in from the sea; they broke and shared their bread together and drank retsina from the barrel. Their living faith had spilled into every action of their lives. It showed in their faces. It was like an embryo of things unseen, infinitely humble; yet of eschatological dimension.

The owner of the cafe had a smile partly blacked out by missing teeth, he finished the dregs from his customers' glasses, bending over backwards and crossing himself in a ritual that became mechanical by mid morning.

For some reason he seemed to like us, there was no exchange of words but he pointed a finger indicating that we must stay, while he disappeared out of the darkness into the bright sunlight.

'He's gone to the market,' someone said. 'He'll bring you a fish.'

A few minutes later he came in carrying a package. There was no fish. His toothless smile was wider than ever and he had a wicked gleam of secrecy in his eyes. Inside the package was a pile of strawberries which he tipped on to a cracked enamel plate. He then stretched for a bottle which was hidden on a very high shelf. The label on the bottle was covered in brown corrugated paper. It was obviously something very precious to him for he kissed it like an icon. He then poured over the scarlet strawberries a clear liquid from the bottle and stirred. The strawberries were unwashed, they still had their green husks on them, and dust and bruises from the market.

'It's alright' said a Greek. 'That liquid will kill the germs quicker than any insecticide.'

He then kissed the bottle again and replaced it on the top shelf. With love and enormous reverence he put the cracked enamel plate with the strawberries in front of us and with his arms crossed over his chest, like waiting for the Eucharist, he watched while we ate.

Whether the molton liquid was vodka or raw alcohol we never knew. We shared a strange sacrament. Then he turned into the darkness of the room and crossed himself again.

Some months later I was told that the cafe came under new management and was to be modernized. Neon lights – shiny tables. The old man tied a heavy stone on to a rope and wound it around his waist. Then he just walked into the sea.

On the morning before Charlotte's funeral Sarah and I had stood beside her coffin, alone in the flower-filled scented chancel of the Church. We knew of the love and tears that the girls from the flowershop had woven into a cross of daisies and white rosebuds lying on the coffin. Now it was to symbolize our tears. Our despair. Then, unexpectedly, unmistakably, a great peace came into us and grew to an unbelievable stillness and joy.

When the Holy Spirit comes upon us we are assured with a certainty, beyond logic and beyond words, that there is no place or situation where God cannot enter with His transforming love.

Intent Only on Life describes the conversion of William Barlow, who as an instructor in the Irish Guards found in the ascetism of army discipline an extraordinary parallel to faith in the Eastern Orthodox Church. Religious concepts which had once been lifeless gradually took on life. In its disciplined environment, its economy of movement, sobriety and degree of obedience the army was comparable to monastic training.

Seeing beyond the romantic beauty which is often the first thing you notice in Orthodoxy, he describes its vastness of vision 'the expanse of life with something of cosmic dimensions.' So completely different from Western Christian upbringing.

Although I reviewed the book for *The Tablet* in November 1991 I have found even more depth, particularly in the final chapter ending with *Stavronikita*. This is the gradual stripping away before the whole mystery of the Incarnation and The Kingdom can be perceived. The glory, no longer hidden in the darkness becomes 'visible'.

I include these excerpts for the marvellous observation and unexpected imagery in the Byzantine eccentricity of Mount Athos.

... 'Try this' (said the young monk from Athens), pouring some water for me, and awaiting my reaction. Like all Greek water, it was delicious and very cold. 'How old?' he asked.

It tasted fresh and I said so.

'Of course,' he snapped back, without actually calling me stupid. 'But how old?'

Oh well, I thought, I'd better humour him ...

'A week?'

'A week! A week!' he repeated gleefully, beginning to look quite mad.

'All right, then, a month!'

'Ah ha! Not a week, my friend. Not a month. Not even a year, my friend.'

'Oh?'

'No. Shall I tell you?'

'You had better.'

He waited a moment and all his agitation went. Quietly, as though letting me in on a family secret, he said:

'My friend, the water you have just tasted was blessed at the foundation of this monastery.'

'But that was in the fourteenth century!'

'Thirteenth,' he countered. 'Do you believe that?'

'If you say so.'

'Good. Wait here.' With that he again disappeared, slamming the door behind him. Once more quietness returned to the delightful room. Not for long. Soon he was back this time carrying a small plastic phial with some cellotape wound about it.

'Now then, take some away with you and drink it in fifty years' time, in a hundred even, and you will discover it will still be fresh.'

WILLIAM BARLOW

Intent Only on Life

Father Dometios and I had been walking for some time without either of us saying anything when he suddenly reached down and pulled something out of the ground. He shook the earth from it, and I saw it was a bone. 'It belonged to one of the fathers of the monastery, long since dead. They used to bury them here.' He flung it down and we moved on, once again in silence. We were quite high now and I could see the monastery below. Outside its walls was an abandoned tractor looking somewhat incongruous beside the ancient buildings. Yet again he swooped downwards and retrieved something from the ground. Some seeds. We stopped and he handed them to me. 'Take them as a memorial of me,' he said. 'As a memorial of me ...' That was straight out of the New Testament. So was *Eucharist* – the Greek word for 'thank you'. The Greeks, I noticed, besides quoting the Gospel, incorporated its words and phrases into their very language, that it came out in their conversation naturally. I liked it. We walked on again, quite high up now, until we came to a large, flat topped stone which would have been ideal for human sacrifice. Was he going to tell me that this was where Abraham had brought Isaac for sacrifice?

'This is where I come at night to pray. I lie here and look up at the sky. Sometimes aircraft fly overhead and wink at me.'

'Navigation lights, Father.'

'Maybe. But they wink at me all the same.'

WILLIAM BARLOW

Intent Only on Life

I imagine Father Dometios must be dead now, though you never can tell. Atrocious food, appalling hygiene, little sleep, unrelieved mind-numbing routine, and hours spent indoors without exercise lengthen life wonderfully. So if you were to tell me he was still alive and well, I would believe it. I hope he is, because I would be happy to think others could meet him as I did and bring him news of the world he so dearly loved and had never been able to forget. Or even wanted to, I'll wager.

My reason for seeking him out was that I had heard he was hospitable and spoke English. Getting monks to talk at all on Athos, in any language, was a problem. Understandably so. Why should men who had renounced the world to be alone want to be pestered by people whom they would never see again and who could be depended upon only for their curiosity? All they would do is ask silly, superficial questions and then treat lightly what they were told, 'What about miracles?' I asked a monk in a spirit of genuine inquiry, for strange things were said to have happened on Athos. 'The most amazing thing I have ever seen,' replied the monk in mild rebuke, 'is this poor monastery feeding people like you every day, all the year round. Truly, that is a miracle.'

WILLIAM BARLOW
Intent Only on Life

Supper that evening was inedible. There were no other visitors, so when the meal was over I went back to my own room. There was quite some time to go before the night-long service began, and it would have been sensible to get some sleep in first. But there was a storm raging outside and it thrilled me to sit alone in the dark and look out into the wild night, trying to visualize the breakers below. Offshore, I could see the lights of a small cluster of fishing boats riding out the storm. Because of the lightening, I stood at the window as a celebrity might stand before a battery of cameras in eager glimpses of the boats and saw the silhouetted land mass on the horizon, more substantial now and less distant-looking than in the daytime.

WILLIAM BARLOW

Intent Only on Life

Several times on Athos I received the fleeting intuition that prayer was a form of warfare and that it had a cosmic dimension involving the elements. These moments of insight had always come when appreciating the great beauty of the Athonite scenery. The landscape was always idyllically peaceful whilst the sea was invariably becalmed, as if exhausted after battle. Was there a connection between the prayer life, with the singing of the offices throughout the night when the world was asleep, and the almost disturbing tranquillity of the scenery by day? Was it that some great cosmic clash had taken place?

When the sound of bells and the vigorous striking of the semantron like Drake's drum beating, signalled it was time for church, the storm was still raging. The monastery seemed under siege, as if the stand-to were being sounded to repel a final, desperate assault on the walls by hostile forces.

WILLIAM BARLOW
Intent Only on Life

The monastery was too poor to be lit by many candles and everything around me was absorbed into the black background. I assumed that the monks were there, although I could not see them and I already knew myself to be the only visitor. I went forward as solitary as a survivor from a wrecked ship, as one who had been miraculously saved, positioning myself beside a wall amidst the whole company of heaven invisibly present on the richly decorated interior. A voice came from somewhere to my front, presumably behind the iconostasis, and was immediately answered from the body of the church. I searched around and saw the camouflaged features of a monk's bearded face, his position given away by a combination of light and movement. In his hand there was a candle which dripped grease onto the book from which he was reading. The long night service had begun. I knew more or less what to expect by now and I was not disappointed. The two monks got into their stride, scooping up the psalms and swallowing Scripture like spaghetti. The pace never once flagged and it quickly became monotonous. I wondered what its purpose could possibly be and refused to believe there was any, not at that speed or for that long. Fancy doing that for the rest of your life, I thought! There must be other ways of becoming holy!

WILLIAM BARLOW

Intent Only on Life

The church had taken on the mien of a photographer's darkroom. As light returned to the world and filtered slowly into the building, everything began to acquire definition. The golden smears of the saints' haloes upon the painted walls were first upon the scene and waited patiently to adorn their heroes. One by one, emperors, virgins, hesychasts, hermits, desert fathers, stylites, soldiers, bishops, confessors and martyrs stepped forth out of the gloom as though in answer to their names on an early-morning roll call. All seemed intent upon the service.

The night was now fully past and nothing in the church remained hidden. The whole economy of salvation stood revealed in the rich, startling, Byzantine imagery of the Gospel story and the tradition of the Church emblazoned like battle honours on every pillar and wall. In the golden interior of the cupola overhead the Pantocrator reigned supreme. I looked down, expecting to see the monk. He was still there, completing his prayer.

The image, though, had changed. When I looked at him I no longer saw a monk. Somehow, he seemed to have transcended the image so that it was only by seeing him as a man that I could capture his stature. Once more the image of monastic aloneness presented itself, only now it was the aloneness of a stupendous emancipation where Man emerges from the illusions of a false identity. In this celebration of freedom there was neither monk, nor priest, neither Greek nor even Orthodox – nothing, in fact, which could detract from the glory of God which is Man fully realized.

WILLIAM BARLOW

Intent Only on Life

Creation and Beauty

It is thou who hast made the heavens and the earth by thy great power and by thy outstretched arm! Nothing is too hard for thee.

(JEREMIAH 32.17)

Colour is very important in the Orthodox Tradition, both in the icon and in the religious architecture. The white paint on the walls of a Church has been described as a virgin dressed in white. Dionysius the Areopagite called white the symbol of godliness, sincerity and tranquillity. The golden cupola crowning the white Church emphasises Christ as the Head. Gold, with its value, its nobility and 'likeness to the sun guaranteed that the precious metal would make an early appearance in Christian history.'*
The circle of the dome, without beginning or end is complete in itself. 'God in the world, Jesus Christ, Heaven reaching down to earth.'

In Greece we see the rounded Dome as deep blue – for the sky, for Heaven – *oupavos*. It is simple and beautiful and makes a strong statement without further explanation.

*Archimandrite Longin of Dusseldorf

A Russian Orthodox Baptism

My infant grandchildren Alexander and Xenia were christened in the Russian Orthodox Cathedral in London. There is more stillness in Russian spirituality than in the Greek but in this Cathedral the darkness and the candlelight dramatically illuminate the action. One is conscious of an almost Cosmic Light and Darkness – Good and Evil in the eternal battle of principalities and powers. The words, both in Slavonic and English are of a strange primordial poetry, giving the Holy Baptism an enormity of depth and mystery. There is a hugeness in the event. It is awesome. Images remain. The baby holding his arms outstretched against his mother, in the shape of a cross. Unintended, like an innocent witness waiting to receive the whole magnitude of the Christian faith. One finds this in Orthodoxy, the unexpected symbolism, again and again, making you comprehend things that are beyond words. The baby is held high, dripping with the Baptismal water – the water catching the light, shining in the light. A Second Birth, of water and light.

This darkness and light continues throughout the Baptism. The words are powerful, calling down the Holy Spirit. The first long prayer is to the Greatness of God, a hymn to his wonders.

> For thou, of thine own good will, has brought into being all things which before were not, and by thy might thou uphold-est creation and by thy providence thou orderest the world ... The sun singeth unto thee. The moon glorifieth thee. The stars meet together before thy presence. The light obeyeth thee. The deeps tremble before thee. The Angelic Powers serve thee. The Choirs of the Archangels fall down in adoration before thee. The many-eyed Cherubim and the six-winged Seraphim, as they stand round about and fly, veil their faces in awe before thine ineffable glory. For thou, who art God inex-pressible, existing uncreated before the ages ... . For we have called upon thy Name, O Lord, and it is wonderful, and glorious, and terrible unto adversaries.

With the exorcism that follows Satan doesn't have a chance!

> Let all adverse powers be crushed beneath the sign of the image of thy cross.
>
> We pray thee, O God, that every aerial and obscure phantom may withdraw itself from us; and that no demon of darkness may conceal himself in this water; and that no evil spirit which instilleth darkest of intentions and rebelliousness of thought may descend into it with him who is about to be baptised ...

The baby is anointed 'with the oil of gladness' and then plunged into the water three times and held high between each immersion.

Afterwards the Priest sprinkles him with pure water.

'Thou are baptized. Thou art illumined. Thou art sanctified ...' The baby is changed into a white garment – clothed with 'the robe of righteousness.'

A Greek Orthodox Baptism

The first thing I had to adjust to was seeing a priest roll up his sleeves and test the water with his elbow at an infant baptism. What a contrast, I thought, between his workmanlike approach and the uncertainty about their role which was afflicting many of the clergy in England. There was nothing half hearted about the baptism, either. Not only was the babe fully immersed in the font, but the godparents took a hand by smothering its head with the baptismal waters.* Then the priest, raising the infant to arm's length above him, invoked the Trinity in a loud voice, plunging the babe into the water between the naming of each Person. The baby's response was spirited. Each time it was lifted up, it laughed, bringing applause and gleeful cheers from everyone present. This was all so human and spontaneous that I could not help joining in, nor would I hold back the tears of joy at seeing the babe held aloft in the name of God, wet and dripping as though newly emerged from the womb . . .

WILLIAM BARLOW

Intent Only on Life

*This is actually oil which has been blessed and is wiped over the head and sometimes over the body of the baby, by the Godparents.

147

The Mother of God trusted you might say madly, blindly, insanely at the conception of God into her womb. We try hard and continue to follow her example of the joy of believing and yet not knowing, and the piercing agony of watching her Son crucified day after day, hour after hour, and forever asking her question, 'How shall this be?'

'Be humble and you will remain whole, be bent and you will remain straight ... Appear plainly and hold to simplicity.' Our artistic and Christian attitude must be what, for want of better words, I would call 'the poverty of innocence.' ...

The one thing, the only thing that can save us is simplicity and this simplicity leads to the last revolution left to our civilization – the Beatitudes of Christ. In their 'foolishness' they speak to a tragic world, that prefers Ceasar to God, which amounts to a condemnation of God in favour of 'the World'.

In the magnificent event of the Incarnation the doors have once again been opened for Heaven and Earth to be joined.

In the Beatitudes we are invited to turn the world upside down. The time has come when we simply have to choose between God and Mammon, before it is too late.

JOHN TAVENER

In thy Kingdom remember us, O Lord, when thou comest into thy Kingdom. Blessed are the poor in spirit: for theirs is the kingdom of heaven. Blessed are they that mourn: for they shall be comforted. Blessed are the meek: for they shall inherit the earth. Blessed are they that do hunger and thirst after righteousness: for they shall be filled. Blessed are the merciful: for they shall obtain mercy. Blessed are the pure in heart: for they shall see God. Blessed are the peacemakers: for they shall be called the children of God. Blessed are they which are persecuted for righteousness' sake: for theirs is the kingdom of heaven. Blessed are ye when men shall revile you, and persecute you, and shall say all manner of evil against you falsely, for my sake.

Rejoice, and be exceeding glad:
for great is your reward in heaven.

THE BEATITUDES

We must form the souls of our children. A child born and growing up today is even more disadvantaged than were his parents. Without careful effort and concern, his parents cannot prevent him from being crippled in soul and stunted in spirit. It is important for adults to strive for the elevation and purity of their souls; it is even more urgent to see that the idealism, the spiritual quickness, the simplicity and the single-heartedness of a child's soul is offered the very best sustenance possible. Children who are sustained on the best in music, reading, and art will develop a genuineness of instinct, a surety of spiritual ear, which will be invaluable throughout their lives. They learn not to be fooled by cheapness, and they will never forget the images of purity, chivalry, integrity and beauty they gained from reading and listening to the very best the human heart and mind have to offer. When their souls are well formed, they will be able to withstand many of the delusions and shallow mockeries which will await them in the world.

SISTERS OF ST XENIA'S SKETE

(suggested to me by Lillian Delevoryas (Amis))

The Song of Simeon was like a sunset in which a shadow heralds a substance ...

Simeon said:

'This child is destined to be a sign which men reject; and you too shall be pierced to the heart. Many in Israel will stand or fall because of him.' Luke (2.34)

It was as if the whole history of the Divine Child were passing before the eyes of the old man. Every detail of that prophecy was to be fulfilled within the lifetime of the Babe. Here was a hard fact of the Cross, affirmed even before the tiny arms of the Babe could stretch themselves out straight enough to make the form of a cross. The child would create terrible strife between good and evil, stripping the masks from each, thus provoking a terrible hatred. He would be at once a stumbling block, a sword that would divide evil from good, and a touchstone that would reveal the motives and dispositions of human hearts. Men would no longer be the same once they had heard His name and learned of His life. They would be compelled either to accept Him, or reject Him. About Him there would be no such thing as compromise. Only acceptance or rejection, resurrection or death. He would, by His very nature, make men reveal their secret attitudes toward God.

Simeon was practically calling Him the 'Divine Disturber', who would provoke human hearts either to good or evil.

FULTON J SHEEN

The Life of Christ

Salvation is extended to the whole of God's creation. St Isaac the Syrian sees life in all of God's handiwork, the animals, the trees, the rocks. He writes thus, 'When a man with such a heart as this thinks of the creatures and looks at them, his eyes are filled with tears because of his overwhelming compassion that presses upon his heart. The heart of such a man grows tender; and he cannot endure to hear of or to look upon any injury, even the smallest suffering, inflicted upon anything in creation. Therefore he never ceases to pray with tears even for the dumb animals, for the enemies of truth and for all who do harm to it, asking that they may be guarded and receive God's mercy. And for the reptiles also he prays with a great compassion, which rises up like this:

> Wherever you turn your eyes, there is God's symbol;
> Wherever you read, you will find there his types ...
> Look and see how Nature and Scripture are linked together ...
> Praise for the Lord of Nature,
> Glory for the Lord of Scripture.

FATHER BARNABAS

'Everything drew me to love and thank God; people, trees, plants, animals – I saw them all as my kinsfolk, I found in them all the magic of the Name of Jesus.'

The Way of a Pilgrim

As we grow in grace we grow in kinship with Nature. If we believe Christ's words 'I am the Way, the Truth and the Life' (John 14.6) then where there is Life there is Christ. If also we believe that 'God is love' (1 John 4.8), and we know that love certainly exists in animals, then there is something of God in them, which will transcend death. How all this will happen we do not know, but we are content to leave this as a mystery in the hands of a loving Life-Giver.

FATHER BARNABAS

O God, enlarge within us the sense of
fellowship with all living things,
our brothers the animals to whom thou
gavest the earth as their home in
common with us.

We remember with shame that in the past
we have exercised the high dominion
of man with ruthless cruelty
so that the voice of the earth,
which should have gone up to thee
in song, has been a groan of travail.

May we realize that they live not for
us alone but for themselves and for
thee, and that they love the
sweetness of life.

St Basil the Great

(suggested to me by Ilyas Haritakis)

For those, O Lord,
the humble beasts,
that bear with us
the burden and heat of the day,
and offer their guileless lives
for the well-being of humankind;
and for the wild creatures,
whom Thou hast made
wise, strong, and beautiful,
we supplicate for them
Thy great tenderness of heart,
for Thou hast promised to save
both man and beast,
and great is Thy loving kindness,
O Master,
Saviour of the world.

ST BASIL THE GREAT

(suggested to me by Ilyas Haritakis)

When I consider thy heavens, the work of thy fingers, the moon
and the stars, which thou hast ordained.
What is man, that thou art mindful of him? And the son of man,
that thou visitest him?
For thou hast made him a little lower than the angels, and hast
crowned him with glory and honour.
Thou madest him to have dominion, over the works of thy hands:
thou hast put all things under his feet:
All sheep and oxen, yea, and the beasts of the field;
The fowl of the air, and the fish of the sea, and whatsoever
passeth through the paths of the seas.
O Lord our Lord, how excellent is thy name in all the earth!

(PSALM 8.3–9)

My book is the whole visible creation, and it lies open before me. Whenever I wish to read in it the words of God.

ANTHONY THE GREAT

Sometimes I have come to understand theological and difficult truths in a way that words could never explain. The stem of a jasmine, for instance is unremarkable in itself, like dull green wire, yet it contains such potential beauty, clusters of green leaves with white five petalled scented flowers that are sheer magic. I began to grasp the potential held in all of us. The past, the present, and the future were already implicit. This led me to seeing Time, not simply as finite, but in its full eternal dimension.

Isaac of Syria, perhaps the greatest among the ascetic and mystical writers of Eastern Christianity, speaks of this immense compassion which takes hold of a heart that approaches the summit of perfection. 'What is a compassionate heart?' he asks, and he answers:

> It is a kindling of the heart for all creation — for mankind, the birds, the animals, even the enemies of the truth and for all that is. And when he thinks of them or contemplates them, tears stream from his eyes because of the power of mercy which moves his heart with great compassion. And the heart feels itself touched, and he cannot endure to see or hear a creature suffer any harm, even the slightest pain. And he offers then, even for those who hurt him, continuous prayers and tears, that they might be saved and strengthened. Even for those that creep in the dust does he pray — out of the immense compassion which is poured out into his heart without measure, following the example of God.

NICHOLAS ARSENIEV

Revelation of Life Eternal

As prophets, our vocation is to seek out the words of God which are hidden within each thing, from stone to angel. By these divine words or *logoi* God brought each thing into existence and keeps it in existence, and gives it its unique role in the cosmic symphony. Taken together, all these words are also a poem of love written by the Divine Lover of man to woo us, to reveal to us something of His beauty beyond words.

We are priests because the whole creation has its purpose beyond itself, in God, and so needs a mediator who is united both to it and to God. Genuine human culture therefore culminates in the liturgical act of us offering bread and wine in the Eucharist. There Christ performs His divine culture and transforms our offering into His own Body and Blood, and we partake of Him. Our sacrifice is not to simply return to God the raw materials of wheat and grapes, like the foolish steward who merely gave back the one talent entrusted him. Rather, we offer creation transformed by our labours. The purpose of God's descent in Christ is fulfilled when we ascend by offering ourselves and all creation; the world becomes sacrament.

Our third ministry, kingship, is not freedom to tyrannise our kingdom, but the God-given ability to lead it towards the King of kings. Such spiritual sovereignty can be likened to a team of skilful spinners, weavers and embroiderers, who are commissioned to make a garment fit for a queen – in our case, the Bride of Christ. By their artistic mastery these craftsmen unveil and articulate the *logos* of each of their materials. But in spiritual artistry the process does not end there. When the Bride is united to Christ and is transfigured – shines with the uncreated light of God – then her garment, the sanctified cosmos, shines with it.

BROTHER AIDAN

The temptation to get 'hooked' on beauty and forget to move on is a real danger; nevertheless, as a stepping stone to the heart of the mysteries, it is enormously helpful. The early fathers of the church, who had a deep knowledge of human psychology, understood this well, especially St John Chrysostom whose Liturgy the Orthodox still celebrate today. He knew that for ordinary mortals to enter into the sublime realm of the spirit preparation is necessary. Our hardened hearts must be made maleable – the wax must be melted for the impression to take. The Liturgy does this by feeding us at every level – sight, sound, smell, taste; and for the mind, the divine food of the Word of God, progressing from the Old to the New Testament, and culminating in the Gospel.

One is taken from the outer world of material concerns, and gradually brought to the point of receiving the spirit through the sacrament of communion.

LILLIAN DELEVORYAS (AMIS)

Beauty, like all other aspects of art, was once an aspect of the absolute Truth, which was God. Therefore, a thing was beautiful in proportion to its faithfulness in reflecting some part of the image and truth of God. Now, having lost the concept of Truth, we no longer have a true concept of Beauty, and feed on mediocrity, on ugliness, on anti-beauty, anti-heroes, anti-art, the mockery of God and man.

We must learn again what beauty is.

We must feel again that pang of homesickness, that bittersweet joy at almost touching, yet never grasping, almost hearing, yet never catching, Him Whose Beauty makes art beautiful. In its truest, deepest sense, that is what art does; that is why we need it. It continually whets a thirst it cannot quench, continually reminds us of a hunger it cannot satisfy. It leads us up to the very highest reaches of human experience, and then leaves us still homesick, still longing for we know not what, and at that point the spirit is enabled to go on, to find its true home in God.

SISTERS OF ST XENIA'S SKETE

(*suggested to me by Lillian Delevoryas (Amis)*)

Speaking of the Kingdom

'Very early in the morning ... at the rising of the sun', they brought 'sweet spices, that they might come and anoint Him.' That they might anoint Christ's body, that they might treat with reverence the material body of the immaterial God. In the tenderness and respect they showed towards matter, they were 'preaching the Gospel to all creation'. And they were able to do so because the love of Christ had filled the whole of their being.

Let us follow their example. And may our love of Christ, the Son of God become the Son of Man, lead us to reverence the material world which He created as a body for Himself, and may we be enabled thereby to bring the Gospel, the 'good news' of the coming of God's Kingdom, to every creature and to all creation.

Christ, after the Resurrection, tells his disciples to 'go into all the world, and preach the Gospel to every creature.' ... And what a responsibility this is. It means struggling not to export our fallenness into the rest of creation. To avoid creating ugliness by letting our hands, as we legitimately use the goodness of this world, create beauty instead ...

In these words of Christ therefore is to be found the heart of an Orthodox 'ecology', for our task is not just to create a world in which man and other creatures can be at home, truly at home, but to create a world in which God can feel at home alongside us: a world in which our labours reflect the beauty of the Triune deity: a world in which even man's works give praise to God and 'exalt Him above all for ever.'

BISHOP BASIL OF SERIEVO

Our failure to perceive the divine in man has gone hand in hand with a failure to perceive the divine in nature. As we have dehumanized man, so we have desanctified nature . . .

By the phrase, 'the desanctification of nature', I refer to that process whereby the spiritual significance and understanding of the created world has been virtually banished from our minds, and we have come to look upon things and creatures as though they possessed no sacred or numinous quality.

For man is called upon to mediate between heaven and earth, between God and His Creation. But when he closes his consciousness to what is above it, he obstructs that flow through which material things may be saturated by the spirit or the spirit may become incarnate, and the result is a disorder in creation which brutalizes both man and nature. Because it is only through man fulfilling his role as mediator between God and the World that the World itself can fulfil its destiny and be transfigured in the Light and presence of God.

PHILIP SHERRARD

The Rape of Man and Nature

When our human nature lay fallen upon the earth it looked towards the serpent and held its image. But now that it has arisen and looks towards the good, turning its back on sin, it takes on the form of the good towards which it faces. For it looks now upon that archetypal Beauty — for that is the Dove. For, turning towards the light, it has been made into the image of light, and within this light it has taken on the lovely form of the Dove — I mean the Dove that symbolizes the presence of the Holy Spirit.

GREGORY OF NYSSA

Glimpses of Glory and Transfiguration

I pray thee O merciful Lord that all the peoples of the
earth may come to know thee by thy Holy Spirit.

SAINT SILOUAN THE ATHONITE

Then I saw a new heaven and a new earth . . .
And the city has no need of sun or moon
to shine upon it, for the glory of God is
the light, and the lamp is the Lamb.

(REVELATION 21)

Christ spoke to the people in the simplest language that all could understand but the content of His talks was realities beyond the grasp of anyone on the planet, even the Apostles; 'Before Abraham was, I am.' 'I and my Father are one.' 'No man knoweth the Son, but the Father; neither knoweth any man the Father, save the Son, and he to whomsoever the Son will reveal him.' 'My Father will love him, and we will come unto him, and make our abode with him.' 'I will pray the Father, and he shall give you another Comforter, that he may abide with you for ever' (John 8.58; 10.30; Matt. 11.27; John 14.23; 14.16).

Here we have a Third Person. How are we to reconcile this with our profound feeling that God is One? Again, the Lord said: 'When the Spirit of truth is come, which proceedeth from the Father, he will guide you into all truth' (John 16.13; 15.26). And He, the Holy Spirit, did come and really does guide us but, as we see, this guidance too, turns out to be a slow process.

ARCHIMANDRITE SOPHRONY

We Shall see Him as He is

One day St Ambrose, Archbishop of Milan, refused to give the sacrament of Communion to Emperor Theodosius because he had ordered the population of Thessalonica to be massacred. The emperor protested and said 'Why should I be rejected when David who was both murderer and an adulterer was not rejected by God?' St Ambrose turned to Emperor Theodosius and said, 'You have imitated David in his crime; now imitate him in his repentance ... In an old legend when an angel came back from earth with a tear of repentance of a vicious looking man intending to harm his fellow humans, God said to the angel, 'Indeed, O angel, you have brought me the most precious thing in the world – the tear of repentance which opens the gates of heaven.'

Diamantis Pateras

Acquire inward peace, and thousands around you will find their salvation.

St Seraphim of Sarov

The Holy Spirit comes when we are receptive. He does not compel. He approaches so meekly that we may not even notice. If we would know the Holy Spirit we need to examine ourselves in the light of the Gospel teaching, to detect any other presence which may prevent the Holy Spirit from entering into our souls. We must not wait for God to force Himself on us without our consent. God respects and does not constrain man. It is amazing how God humbles Himself before us. He loves us with a tender love, not haughtily, not with condescension. And when we open our hearts to Him we are overwhelmed by the conviction that He is indeed our Father. The soul then worships in love.

ARCHIMANDRITE SOPHRONY
His Life is Mine

... the action of the Holy Spirit cannot be defined verbally. It has to be lived and experienced directly.

BISHOP KALLISTOS OF DIOKLEIA

The Holy Spirit gives all things, makes prophecies flow, perfects priests, teaches wisdom to the unlettered, reveals fishermen to be theologians, welds together the whole order of the Church. Advocate, consubstantial and sharing the same throne with the Father and the Son, glory to you!

FROM VESPERS FOR THE FEAST OF PENTECOST

(suggested to me by Archbishop Gregorios)

In his great love God was unwilling to restrict our freedom, even though he had the power to do so. He has left us to come to him by the love of our heart alone.

ISAAC OF NINEVEH

God's love is by its nature warmth. When it lights on someone without any limit, it plunges the soul into ecstasy. That is why the heart of one who has felt it cannot bear to be deprived of it. But he gradually undergoes a strange alteration in proportion to the love that enters into him.

ISAAC OF NINEVEH

Ascetic Treatises

St Seraphim of Sarov is one of the most beloved Saints in the Russian Orthodox Church. His cell – or 'desert' – was in a dense pine wood, on the bank of the river Sarovka. From his teachings and from the many stories about his life in the forest, this is perhaps the best known.

From The Conversation with N.A. Motovilov
– on Light.

Remember Moses after his intercourse with God on Mount Sinai. People could not look at him, so radiant was his face with supernatural light. He even had to appear before the people with a veil covering his features. Remember the transfiguration of our Lord on Mount Tabor. A great radiance enveloped Him. 'His garments became shining and exceeding white as snow, and his disciples fell upon their face and were very much afraid.' And when, in that light, Moses and Elias appeared to Him, then, in order to shield the disciples from the blinding light of Divine Grace, a 'cloud overshadowed them.' And in the same way the Grace of the all-holy Spirit of God appears, clothed in ineffable light, to all to who God reveals His action.

G.P. FEDOTOV (ED.)

A Treasury of Russian Spirituality

'But how,' I asked Father Seraphim, 'shall I know I abide in the Grace of God's Holy Spirit?'

'This ... is very simple,' he answered, 'wherefore our Lord says: "All things are simple to those who have understanding."' The Apostles always knew whether or not the Spirit of God was with them; penetrated by Him, and aware of His indwelling with them, they said with conviction that their task was holy and pleasing to our Lord God ... 'What else do you want, good Father?'

'What I want,' I said, 'is to understand this completely.'

Then Father Seraphim took me firmly by the shoulders and said to me: 'Right now, good Father, we are both in the Spirit of God. Why, then, do you not look at me.'

I said: 'I cannot look at you, Father ... Your face has become brighter than the sun, and my eyes ache.'

Father Seraphim said: 'Fear nothing, God-loving one. You too have become as radiant as I. You yourself are now in the fullness of the Divine Spirit, or else you could not see me as I appear to you.'

G.P. FEDOTOV (ED.)

A Treasury of Russian Spirituality

The Uncreated Light

After His resurrection Christ appeared exclusively to those who were capable of apprehending Him in His now divinized and translucent flesh, and remained invisible to everyone else. Thus the uncreated Light stays unseen for those who do not seek to know God with all their being. And again, another curious analogy with physical light – it, too, is invisible without an object to catch and reflect it. Nature in the light of the earthly sun is a splendid sight for the eye. But the Divine Light, when it irradiates man, in a marvellous way transfigures him. The most ordinary individual, apparently disfigured by sin, in his prayer of repentance is illumined by Light and looks young and even beauteous.

ARCHIMANDRITE SOPHRONY
We Shall see Him as He is

Experience shows all too clearly that once we Christians start reducing the scope of the revelation given to us by Christ and the Holy Spirit, we gradually cease to be attracted by the Light made manifest to us.

ARCHIMANDRITE SOPHRONY
His Life is Mine

'God is light,' says St Simeon, 'and he communicates his brightness to those who are united with him, to the extent that they are purified.'

'I have often seen the light,' says St Simeon, 'sometimes it has appeared to me within myself, when my soul possessed peace and silence, sometimes it has appeared only at a distance, and at times it was even hidden completely. Then I experienced great affliction, believing that I would never see it again. But from the moment when I began to shed tears, when I bore witness to a complete detachment from everything, and to an absolute humility and obedience, the Light appeared once again, like the sun which dissipates the thickness of the clouds and reveals itself little by little bringing joy.'

These are the realities of the age to come which can be glimpsed here below — in ecstasy at first, but in a constant communion with the divine in those who are more nearly perfect.

VLADIMIR LOSSKY
The Vision of God

The Lord appeared to St Silouan at the outset of his monastic life. Only a few months after he entered the cloister the Lord was manifest to him in great Light (a happening that I tried to describe in my book about him). It was then that he knew God through the Holy Spirit, then that it was given to him to delight in Christ's indescribable humility, then that he began to pray for the whole world as for himself. It would be superfluous to point out that this spiritual grace goes far beyond the confines of human ethics; that to St Silouan it was given to live in the sphere of this Light, to breathe the air of the upper world.

A frequent occurrence on Mt Athos is to see a monk entirely in God, in Light, and the Light in him. But he has no intellectual reaction – it seems to him a natural state to be in.

ARCHIMANDRITE SOPHRONY

We Shall see Him as He is

The soul which, after much striving and seeking, has touched the abundant fullness, is flooded with joy ... For all that it deemed of worth hitherto is as nothing, beside what it now experienced and knows what now permeates it and dominates it with incomparable majesty, with overwhelming might and beauty ... The soul has touched the 'wells of living water', has drunk eagerly of them, and received a new, eternal life.

This is that costly pearl which it is said that the merchant who found it sold all to possess it; this is that treasure in the field of which it is said that the man who found it sold all his possessions and bought that field ... Paul speaks of the 'unsearchable riches of Christ' of the 'riches of the glory of this mystery which is Christ in you,' of the 'treasure' which men carry about in 'earthen vessels'. 'Be filled with the Spirit,' cries Paul.

NICHOLAS ARSENIEV

Mysticism and the Eastern Church

Glimpses of Glory

When we experience the presence of the Holy Spirit in us, how can we describe what we feel? Immobilized physically perhaps, yet with our soul quickened in some way, able to understand things, grasp things, that our worldly minds would not be able to do. But we are enfolded in a peace and joy that is beyond description, for words are inadequate to express such a state of being. We are experiencing His Grace, understanding the Fruits of the Spirit. For some of us it may have taken years of trials and suffering before being able to receive this gift. It may never happen until we have removed from our lives those things that come between us and God. It is 'an encounter with the Absolute', a gradual purifying and stripping of the temple within us in order to accommodate God.

Sarah and I were each given a flower from a parishioner. It is customary to bring flowers for Pentecost in the Orthodox Church and we had none with us. They symbolize the renewal of Nature in Spring, the renewal of mankind through the 'indwelling of the Holy Spirit.'

Mine was a daisy. I looked at my wilting flower. It symbolized too much. My life perhaps. How could God transfigure something so flawed and imperfect. I couldn't hold it and, rather than throw it away, I gave it to Sarah. Hers was less flawed. It hid the imperfection of the flower that I was holding. Then we knelt down for the long, long prayers of Pentecost.

Suddenly I was blinded by glass. In the glass was the reflection of a perfect daisy, each petal intact and shining with immaculate illumination.

Only at the end of the liturgy did I turn round. The huge window in the Cathedral is in the shape of a daisy. The sunlight had shone through with geometric accuracy on to the reflection that had blinded me. I have tried to find and repeat the same set of circumstances on several occasions since, but it has never happened again. It never does. God had given His answer, that He can transfigure anything, however flawed.

I know a man in Christ who fourteen years ago was caught up to the third heaven. Whether it was in the body or out of the body I do not know – God knows. And I know that this man – whether in the body or apart from the body I do not know, but God knows – was caught up to Paradise. He heard inexpressible things, things that man is not permitted to tell.

(2 CORINTHIANS 12.3–4)

The disciple of Abba Silvanus, Sachary, went in and found him in ecstasy with his hands stretched up to heaven. Closing the door he went out. He came back at the sixth and the ninth hour and found him in the same state. At the tenth hour he knocked, went in and found him inwardly at peace. So he said to him, 'How have you been today, Father?' Silvanus replied, 'I was carried up to heaven and saw the glory of God. And I stayed there until just now. And now I am dissolved.'

SILVANUS

Look down from thy holiness on high, O Lord, upon thy people ... Gather us all into thy kingdom. Grant pardon unto those who put their trust in thee ... Purify us by the operation of thy Holy Spirit.

Blessed art thou, O Lord, Master Almighty, who has illumined the day with the light of the sun, and hast made bright the night with the brilliant flashes of lightening.

Govern my life O thou who governest all creation by a word with the unutterable might of thy wisdom ... Hearken unto us from thy holy heaven ... make us worthy of thy kingdom ... cover us with the shelter of thy wings.

A FEW SENTENCES TAKEN FROM
THE LONG PRAYERS AT THE FEAST OF PENTECOST

Christ took Peter, James and John up to a high mountain apart, and was transfigured before them. His face shone as the sun and His raiment became white as light.

The visible sun was eclipsed by the rays of Thy Divinity . . .

Thou wast transfigured upon Mount Tabor O Jesus, and a shining cloud spread out like a tent, covered the apostles with Thy glory. Whereupon their gaze fell to the ground, for thy could not bear to look upon the brightness of the unapproachable glory of Thy face, O Saviour Christ, our God who art without beginning. Do Thou who then hast shone upon them with Thy light, give light now to our souls.

THE FESTAL MENAION

from the Transfiguration of our Lord
Service Book of the Orthodox Church

And the effect of righteousness will be peace, and the result of righteousness, quietness and trust for ever. My people will abide in a peaceful habitation in secure dwellings, and in quiet resting places.

(ISAIAH 32:17–18)

... he has clothed me with the garments of salvation,
he has covered me with the robe of righteousness,
as a bridegroom decks himself with a garland
and as a bride adorns herself with her jewels.
For as the earth brings forth its shoots,
and as a garden causes what is sown in it to spring up,
so the Lord God will cause righteousness and praise
to spring forth before all the nations.

(ISAIAH 61.11)

We all live on the edge of a mystery ... and, from the point of view of its clear apprehension, just outside it.

FATHER EDWARD BOOTH, OP

As we reach the end of the book it is time perhaps to think more deeply about this journey to the Kingdom. The verses from Revelations may seem more relevant than they were at the beginning. The twelve gates of the Holy City are twelve pearls. We know that when an oyster is invaded by a grain of sand 'it secretes a liquid which hardens and then becomes a pearl.' Our entry to the eternal city is through love and perhaps through suffering.

I brought back some white stones which I found by the sea in Greece. They are a pure, almost unearthly white. I keep them in places of prayer in order to remind me of this journey and of the words of Christ in Revelation 2.17:

To him who conquers I will give some of the hidden manna, and I will give him a white stone, with a new name written on the stone which no one knows except him who receives it ...

Christ is Risen! And with Him, He raises fallen Adam. Christ is Risen! And He has raised the human universe. Christ is Risen! And He has filled the universe with fragrance.

We give thanks to the Giver of Life, since He continually grants us the renewal of crosses in this present life. We give praise to the Saviour of the world, since He has enriched us by the gifts of continuous trials, and Who has made us partakers in His unceasing consolation.

You who weep and you who are treated unjustly, you who seek and you who have doubts, take courage! Wait patiently, for He comes in the middle of the night, as did the Bridegroom of life. He rises as the sun from the utter abasement of the Tomb, as Victor over death.

We were waiting to see the end, and it was the beginning that was revealed to us. We have reached the fullness. Now everything is filled with light. All are reconciled in fervent joy. The choirs of Angels and Archangels sing in chorus with the humble, the disgraced, the desperate, the deceased.

VARTHOLOMAEOS

Archbishop of Constantinople and Oecumenical Partriarch

Then I saw a new heaven and a new earth, for the first heaven had passed away, and the sea was no more. And I saw the holy city, new Jerusalem, coming down out of heaven from God, prepared as a bride adorned for her husband, and I heard a loud voice from the throne saying 'Behold the dwelling of God is with men, neither shall there be mourning, nor crying nor pain any more, for the former things have passed away. Behold I make all things new.'

(FROM REVELATION 21)

The city lies foursquare, its length the same as its breadth ... The wall was built of jasper while the city was pure gold, clear as glass. The foundations of the wall of the city were adorned with every jewel; the first was jasper, the second sapphire, the third agate, the fourth emerald, the fifth onyx, the sixth carnelian, the seventh chrysolite, the eighth beryl, the ninth topaz, the tenth chrysophrase, the eleventh jacinth, the twelth amethyst.

And the twelve gates were twelve pearls, each of the gates made of a single pearl, and the street of the city was pure gold, transparent as glass. And the city has no need of sun or moon to shine upon it. For the Glory of God is its Light, and its Lamp is the Lamb.

(FROM REVELATIONS 21)

For blessed is thy Name, and glorified is thy kingdom, of the Father and of the Son, and of the Holy Spirit, now, and ever, and unto ages and ages. Amen.

Sources

Starting the journey

01 A.W. Tozer, *The Knowledge of the Holy* (Cambridge: James Clarke & Co. Ltd.).

02 Archimandrite Sophrony, *We Shall See Him as He is*, by kind permission of the Stavropegic Monastery of Saint John the Baptist.

05 Metropolitan Anthony of Sourozh, *School for Prayer* (Paulist Press).

07 From the Orthodox Prayer Book.

08 Bishop Kallistos of Diokleia, *The Orthodox Way* (New York: St Vladimir's Seminary Press).

09 Cyprian Smith, *The Way of Paradox*, 1987 (London: Darton, Longman and Todd Ltd.) and used by permission of the publishers.

10 This extract is taken from a personal prayer card.

14 Vincent Ferrer Blehl, SJ, *The White Stone: the Spiritual Theology of John Henry Newman* (Massachusetts: St Bede's Publications), pp. 42, 72.

15 Father Lev Gillett, *Encounter at the Well*, 1988 (London: A.R. Mowbray), pp. 14–15. From the end of the Second World War, Fr Gillett was Orthodox chaplain to the Fellowship of St Alban and Sergius for whom this address was given. A prolific writer on Orthodox Spirituality, he died in 1980.

16 This extract is taken from a personal prayer card.

17 Taken from Prayers according to the hours of the day and night: A selection of sentences for each hour.

18 ibid.

19 Reprinted by permission of the State University of New York Press,

from *A Different Christianity*, by Robin Amis © 1995 State University of New York. All rights reserved.

22 Nicodemus of the Holy Mountain (ed., revised by Theophan the Recluse) *Unseen Warfare* (London: A. R. Mowbray), pp. 85, 99, 183.
23 ibid.
24 *Encounter at the Well*, p. 119.
25 Metropolitan Anthony of Sourozh, *Living Prayer*, 1966, 1980 (London: Darton, Longman and Todd Ltd.,) pp. 109–110, 111, and used by permission of the publishers.
26 ibid.
27 Bishop Basil of Serievo, 'Letting down the net' (Luke 5:1–11) from *Speaking of the Kingdom*.
31 *Living Prayer*, pp. 86, 87.
31 George Seaver, *The Faith of Edward Wilson* (London: John Murray Ltd.).
32 Father Barnabas. From one of many papers included in letters.
33 An Evening Prayer in St Antiokh (fifth century) from *A Manual of Eastern Orthodox Prayers*.

The word

42 Taken from *The Service Book of the Orthodox Church*. These are monastic Hours but used by the Orthodox Church at intervals throughout the day.
   In the First Hour we thank God for the light of the day which he has given us, and pray that we may pass the day without sin. According to the ecclesiastical reckoning, the First Hour corresponds with the present seven o'clock in the morning. In the Third Hour we commemorate the Descent of the Holy Spirit upon the Apostles on the day of Pentecost. It corresponds to the present nine o'clock in the morning. In the Sixth Hour, corresponding to twelve o'clock (noon), the Crucifixion of Jesus Christ is commemorated.
   The Ninth Hour, corresponding to three o'clock in the afternoon, commemorates the death of Jesus Christ.
47 Selwyn Hughes, *Every Day with Jesus*, January and February 1996 (Surrey: CWR Ltd.).
47 ibid.

Spiritual struggle

Love

and Bible Scholar. Superintendent at the Bethesda Leprosy Hospital in Narsapur, India for twenty five years.

94 Robert Barnes was Deputy Head of St John's College School, Cambridge.

96 Nicholas Arseniev, *Revelation of Life Eternal* (New York: St Vladimir's Seminary Press).

Death and the immortality of the human soul

105 Prayer of St Thomas More; written in the Tower as he awaited his execution.

106 From *The Lenten Triodion*, translated from the original Greek by Mother Mary and Bishop Kallistos.

111 Constantine Cavarnos, *Modern Greek Philosophers on the Human Soul*, 1967, 1987 (Massachusetts: Institute for Byzantine and Modern Greek Studies), pp. 59, 60, 67, 79. St Nectarios of Aegina, Metropolitan of Pentapolis (1846–1920). The newest saint in Greece, widely known as a miracle worker and healer of disease. He was a prolific writer, poet and mystic.

112 *Modern Greek Philosophers on the Human Soul*, pp. 67, 126.

113 ibid., pp. 53–54.

Places of prayer

115 Catherine de Hueck Doherty, *Poustinia* (Combermere, Ontario, Canada: Madonna House Publications), chapter 1, part I and Chapter 2, part II.

116 Nicholas Arseniev, *Mysticism and the Eastern Church*, 1979 (London: A. R. Mowbray). Evelyn Underhill – a devotional writer of the Anglican Church.

117 Archbishop Pitirim of Volokolamsk (ed.), *The Orthodox Church in Russia* (London: Thames & Hudson Ltd.).
This extract is taken from 'Russian Piety' by Bishop Serafim of Zurich, p. 202.

121 *The Orthodox Church in Russia*.

124 ibid.

128 *A Different Christianity*.

129 ibid.

130 ibid.

131 Thomas Merton, *Thoughts in Solitude* (Tunbridge Wells, Burns & Oates)

135 William Barlow, *Intent Only on Life* (London: HarperCollins Publishers Ltd.).

Creation and beauty

144 *The Orthodox Church in Russia.*

148 John Tavener. Extract from his Westminster Cathedral address for *Art and the End Point.*

149 Taken from the Divine Liturgy.

150 From the article 'Literature, Culture and the Western Soul', first published in *Epiphany Journal.*

151 Fulton J. Sheen, *The Life of Christ* (New York: Bantam Doubleday Dell Publishing Inc.).

154 Andrew Linzey and Tom Regan (eds.), *Compassion for Animals*, 1988 (London, SPCK).

155 ibid.

158 *Revelation of Life Eternal.*

159 Brother Aidan is a monk in The Hermitage of Saints Anthony and Cuthbert, Shrewsbury, Shropshire.

161 From the article 'Literature, Culture and the Western Soul'.

162 Extract from his sermon *Preaching the Gospel to all Creation.*

163 Philip Sherrard, *The Rape of Man and Nature* (Ipswich: Golgonooza Press).

164 Taken from *Glory to Glory*, p. 187.

Glimpses of glory and transfiguration

166 *We Shall See Him as He Is.*

168 Archimandrite Sophrony, *His Life is Mine*, by kind permission of the Stavropegic Monastery of Saint John the Baptist.

169 *The Orthodox Way.*

170 *The Roots of Christian Mysticism.*

171 G.P. Fedotov (ed.), *A Treasury of Russian Spirituality* (London: Sheed & Ward Ltd.).
173 First extract taken from *We Shall See Him as He Is*.
Second extract taken from *His Life is Mine*.
174 Vladimir Losky, *The Vision of God* (St Vladimir's Press), chapter 8.
176 *Mysticism and the Eastern Church*.
178 *The Roots of Christian Mysticism*.
179 Taken from the Orthodox Service Book.
180 Translated from the original Greek by Mother Mary and Bishop Kallistos Ware, 1969, 1984 (London: Faber & Faber Ltd.).
182 Father Edward Booth, OP.
183 Protocol no. 359.